Little Gray Men

*Roswell
and the
Rise of a
Popular
Culture*

✳

little gray men

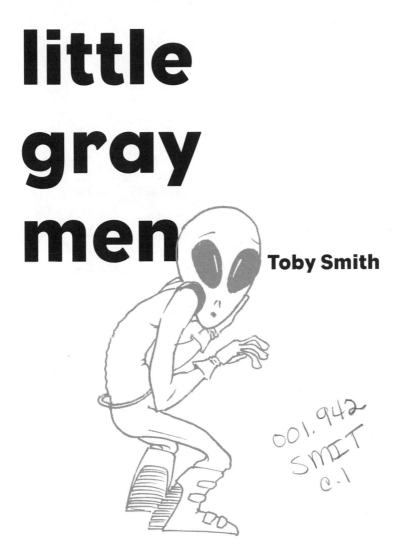

Toby Smith

UNIVERSITY OF NEW MEXICO PRESS
Albuquerque

Illustrations by Aaron Campbell
Design by Susan Walsh
Library of Congress Cataloging-in-Publication Data
Smith, Toby, 1946–
    Little gray men : Roswell and the rise of a popular culture / Toby
Smith. — 1st ed.
      p.   cm.
    Includes bibliographical references.
    ISBN 0-8263-2121-6 (alk. paper)
    1. Unidentified flying objects—Sightings and encounters—New
Mexico—Roswell.   2. Unidentified flying objects in popular culture—
United States.   I. Title.
    TL789.5.N6S65   2000
    001.942'09789'43—dc21   99–27120
                                                            CIP

For my brother, Thomas R. Smith, and in memory of our father, Royall G. Smith. "Look up there, boys. See if you can see Sputnik . . . There it is! Or is that something else?"

1/21/03 Gift

"I got a letter from thirteen-year-old Ryan from Belfast. Now, Ryan, if you're out in the crowd tonight, here's the answer to your question. No, as far as I know, an alien spacecraft did not crash in Roswell, New Mexico, in 1947. And, Ryan, if the United States Air Force did recover alien bodies, they didn't tell me about it either, and I want to know."

—President Bill Clinton, speech in Ireland, 1995

contents

acknowledgments

Much of the research and writing for this book was done in Columbus, Ohio, where I spent three happy months as a James Thurber Journalist-in-Residence.

At The Ohio State University Libraries' Rare Books and Manuscripts room, Elva Griffith and Geoffrey Smith helped me explore one of the largest special collections of UFO literature in the country.

The Thurber House provided a lively place to turn my notes into sentences, and my deepest appreciation is extended to Michael Rosen, Donn Vickers, Jennifer McNally, and Trish Houston.

Gary Kiefer, Mike Harden, Jim Hunter, and Dave Stephenson of *The Columbus Dispatch* contributed a basket of leads and a bunch of inspiration.

Also in Columbus, William E. Jones, a trove of UFO details, pointed me in several directions, all bountiful. Gracias, Bill.

The Columbus Public Library consistently surprised me with its wide range of holdings and its friendly staff. Same goes for Aardvark Video.

In Dayton, Ohio, I am indebted to the public affairs office at Wright-Patterson Air Force Base, in particular Helen Kavanaugh. Air Force historians Rob Young and Bruce Ashcroft aided in my understanding of the public's periodic misunderstanding of things military.

At Dayton's United States Air Force Museum, Dave Menard offered good tips and hearty laughs. Meanwhile, the *Dayton Daily News* came up with a clutch of vital clippings.

In Laramie, Wyoming, Carol L. Bowers of the University of Wyoming's American Heritage Center, unearthed for me the Frank Scully Papers, nearly twenty boxes of significant flying saucer documents saved by a man who seemed to hang onto everything.

In Albuquerque, Leslie Linthicum, John Fleck, and Tony DellaFlora lent gainful assistance through their published articles in the *Albuquerque Journal*. Frank Joyce, a neighbor, never turned me down when I asked if I could drop by and chat about Roswell. The University of New Mexico's Center for Southwest Research, in Zimmerman Library, proved to be a genuine treasure chest.

In Roswell, Sandy and Miles Turner deserve generous praise for graciously opening their home to me. Likewise, Karl Travis and Jim Valdez opened their minds, while Dennis Kelly opened the door for me at Bud's and supplied amiable companionship. The folks who run the UFO Encounter festival, the Roswell Museum and Art Center, the Roswell Public Library, and the Historical Center for Southeast New Mexico patiently answered my many queries. Thanks to all.

In Portales, Jack Williamson pulled out a couple of kitchen chairs and then gave me three hours that he could have spent on his own book.

Fellow journalist Bob Groves, a Roswell observer from afar, delivered crucial bits of advice. Snappy salutes also must go to Angel Rosa and Charles Harness for their cogent long-distance comments.

In his typically gentle but instructive way, David Holtby, associate director of the University of New Mexico Press, furnished unyielding support and essential guidance. To have David as a friend for nearly two decades is to be truly lucky in life.

My wife, Susan, and our sons, Jedediah and Carson, encouraged this project from its early jottings to its final blast-off. My gratitude to them and love for them cannot be calculated.

introduction

"True or untrue, Roswell is seminal."
—*Entertainment Weekly*, 1996

WHEN I WAS A KID growing up in New England, my father periodically spoke of New Mexico. Dad, reared in West Texas, liked to remind me, his occasionally unruly son, that his father regularly threatened to send him to Roswell—to the New Mexico Military Institute—if he didn't shape up. In my father's youth, getting banished to that school apparently was like having to join the French Foreign Legion: Roswell's reputation was of a torrid, desert outpost for the wayward and incorrigible.

For years I feared *I* might be shipped to Roswell. Then, one day, I actually was sent to that city. It was the late 1970s and as a reporter for the *Albuquerque Journal* I went to Roswell to interview a resident who was running for president of the United States. Paul Chalmers Gordon was a blustery, triple-chinned fellow who peddled bumper stickers out of a battered camper truck for a living and who campaigned for office outside public restrooms. His platform? He wanted all taxes repealed, all traitors hanged. He wanted prisoners everywhere pardoned, the Monroe Doctrine restored, and war declared on Israel, Iran, and North Korea. If elected, he planned to move the White House to Springdale, Utah, and set it atop a huge mound of granite, the "world's largest unhewn monolith."

Soon I found I had nothing to fear in Roswell—except maybe Paul Chalmers Gordon. I felt comfortable in Roswell—the town, after all, had been started by a man named Smith, who named it for his father, Roswell Smith, in 1873. Roswell, I decided, was an agreeable place in the Pecos River Valley. Home of one of the nation's most important artesian basins, Roswell was bordered by rows of cotton and corn, crossed with alfalfa fields and fruit orchards, and surrounded by wide stretches of grama grass. "Prettiest little town in the West," Will Rogers had said. With churches on nearly every corner, Roswell was a God-fearing, conservative, patriotic place where every car radio at noon was fixed on the voice of Paul Harvey. I quickly learned how long somebody had been in the community by how he pronounced the town's name. *Rozwill* for newcomers like myself. And, for all others, *Rozzul*.

Nobody in Roswell talked much of UFOs in those days of the late seventies. They mostly talked about moisture (lack of rain) or feed (high prices) or *ky-oats* (predatory carnivori). Oh, now and then when I passed through I would hear the odd mention of space creatures, but usually that was said with a wink of the eye. Then a book came out, in 1980, the first one about the purported UFO crash. However, that book was about as clear as the inside of a blackberry pie. The aliens came and crashed, the book said, and some bodies might have been taken to Ohio, and there might have been another crash somewhere else or maybe two saucers smacked into each other. Who knew?

I had no particular interest in investigating those theories and no overwhelming urge to try to debunk them. I still don't. The Roswell incident was just a wild yarn back then, like the one about Buick-size alligators that lived in a city's sewer system. While on another assignment, this time to Lovington, New Mexico, in July 1995, I had occasion to stop in Roswell on my way home. My waitress at Denny's asked if I was in town with the ewe-eff-owers. *The what?* I replied, not sure what she meant. The UFO fans, she explained, had just come through Roswell to celebrate the forty-eighth anniversary of the Roswell incident. "Wuzzamadder?" she asked with a grin. "Wuddent you a believer?"

I wasn't sure what I believed, but this much was true: I had already been programmed. During the next two years, as the half-century birthday party for Roswell the Incident drew closer, as the hype grew heavier, I suddenly began to have new respect for Paul Chalmers Gordon, bless his singular soul. Paul Chalmers knew what he had in Roswell the Place: a good if sometimes quirky spot to live. My appreciation of Roswell the Place truly grew when I learned during another visit there that NMMI, to which my father was almost sentenced, was not a correctional facility at all but a fine school that trained young men and women to be military officers and at the same time offered a solid education. Indeed, NMMI had turned out the renowned artist Peter Hurd and the two time Pulitzer Prize-winning writer Paul Horgan, both producers of works that I greatly admired. Roger Staubach, whose football heroics I had watched many times on television, attended NMMI before he transferred to the U.S. Naval Academy.

So, as the summer of 1997 beckoned, I decided to spend a week in Roswell, at its UFO Encounter '97. I wanted to see what the hullabaloo was about, I wanted to hear what all the ewe-eff-owers had to say. What I learned was that almost every one of them truly knew that a flying saucer had touched down in Roswell. After all, Roswell offered the "best evidence" of all UFO incidents worldwide. Some people were in town that week to try to disprove the evidence, but they were a definite minority. Of the 40,000 who attended Encounter '97, the For versus Against tally, near as I could figure, stood at 39,966 to 34.

I had to pause and wonder: *Why* were so many people so believing? *Why* did they want to hang onto something that in reality was like trying to cling to a sunbeam? Author Daniel J. Boorstin, once the Librarian of Congress, mulled this question over—way back in 1961. In his ground-breaking book *The Image: A Guide to Pseudo Events in America*, Boorstin wrote, "The American citizen thus lives in a world where fantasy is more real than reality, where the image has more dignity than its original."

As I sat and listened to the guest speakers at Encounter '97, as I gabbed with tourists and year-rounders, even as I bought a souvenir "Alien Dog" T-shirt, I knew there was more to Roswell than simply an alleged crash site, or even alleged crash sites. Roswell had existed long before a flying saucer one dark and stormy night reportedly banged into a ridge northwest of the community. Whether Roswell was substituting fantasy for reality seemed far less significant to me than what Roswell had become. Roswell had served as the launching pad, and continued to be the guiding light, I saw, for almost every societal diversion having to do with UFOs. Roswell was *everywhere*, and that just reinforces the propensity to believe. For instance, Roswell's name is dropped at least a couple of times a year on *The X-Files*. Three times during the 1996-97 television season the show *Dark Skies* featured Roswell-related programs, one of which even blamed Roswell for what happened on that grassy knoll in Dallas.

Because Roswell was the first and only place in this country where the military announced it had fetched a flying saucer—yes, yes, the government later changed its mind and story—Roswell became the Holy Grail, the defining moment in ufology. Simply, Roswell generated an industry of *E.T.*-lovin' folks who wanted nothing more than to be left alone with their bucks and beliefs.

While no one was looking, Roswell also became the embarkation point for every UFO-connected trip taken by the mass media. Roswell became the fiber out of which all flying-saucer stories would henceforth be weaved. From its "little gray men"—that's what Roswell's aliens were called by eyewitnesses, rather than the more familiar "little green men"—sprung a wide assortment of

4

productions: from the goofy *Captain Video* TV show that began in 1949, to a bug-eyed, viridescent four-legged critter on the even goonier *The Simpsons* that came along on television forty years later; from a Broadway play of the 1950s, to *Dick Tracy* comic strips of the 1960s, to a *Playboy* cartoon in the 1990s. The movie *Easy Rider* in 1969 gave us one of the entertainment industry's first mention of Roswell, though to be fair Jack Nicholson didn't actually cite the city by name when he delivered his drug-enhanced, campfire soliloquy:

> That was a UFO beamin' back at ya.
> We was down in Mexico two weeks ago;
> we seen forty of 'em flyin' in formation. They've
> got bases all over the world now, ya know. They've
> been comin' over here since 1946, when the
> scientists first started bouncing radar beams off
> the moon. They have been livin' and workin' among
> us in vast quantities ever since. The government knows
> all about 'em.

In a short humor piece published in *The New Yorker* in 1975 and titled "The UFO Menace," Woody Allen also paid homage to Roswell without actually naming it. Allen's essay featured a letter from a flying saucer buff, I.M. Axelbank, who says, "I am an experienced pilot who was flying my private Cessna from New Mexico to Amarillo, Texas, to bomb some people whose religious persuasions I do not wholly agree with, when I noticed an object flying alongside me. . . ."

Today, it seems as if every "The Truth Is Out There" videocassette popped into a VCR makes a reference to Roswell. Curiously, sometimes those references appear magically. Robin Cook's novel *Invasion* has no mention of Roswell. Yet when the TV movie of the book debuted in 1997, the town's name was inserted into the mouth of an immunologist who explained that an underground confinement room in an extraterrestrial test lab was built "because of Roswell." Jacques Vallee's 1996 novel *Fastwalker*, about alien abduction, doesn't mention Roswell per se, but refers repeatedly to an event in the New Mexico desert in 1947 and a recovered spacecraft. Instantly, we know what event that is. Same with the 1990s television show *The Visitor*. Adam McArthur, that show's lead character, was picked up by a spaceship in 1947 and reared by aliens, in the same manner, I suppose, that wolves are said to sometimes nurture small children lost in the woods. Dropped back down to Earth, The Visitor began to assist folks in distress—every Friday night.

As Roswell leaps out at us in those mediums, a smile crosses our face in recognition. But more than that, the references remind us that Roswell has clout, and thus, we're swayed by that power. At the same time, we brace for additional consumer validation, some of which we know won't be flattering. For example, in its January 1998 issue, *Esquire* magazine gave the city this Dubious Achievement Award: "Calling All Idiots! The Roswell magnet moron turns fifty." In the screamingly satirical 1996 movie *Waiting for Guffman*, we get these lines:

> Everybody thinks that Roswell was the first sighting of a UFO in the United States. And that's bullroar. We had the first sighting here, in 1946. And it wasn't just a sighting. It didn't fly by. They stopped. They landed. And the people in Blaine went on board the ship for a potluck dinner.

So complete is the saturation that the word *Roswell* fills the air, like a necessary element. When people speak of pop culture, they are usually referring to widely read fiction and nonfiction, as well as everything to come along and be heard, written, worn, or seen, including graffiti on a sidewalk. Popular culture is the kind of communication that may be informative but that principally provides pleasure for the participants. Despite what some may think, popular culture is an art form and it appeals to large numbers of people who share similar experiences, interests, values, and tastes.

Just as important, say communications experts Fred Rissover and Richard Birch, is this point: "The mass media are what makes popular culture popular." On a more basic level, the mass media makes pop culture possible. Hence, the mass media and pop culture are inseparably bound, joined tighter, as they say around Roswell, than a tick in a hound dog's ear.

Roswell the Incident was born and bred by the mass media. From its very first breath, in July 1947, when the Associated Press reported in newspapers and radio broadcasts around the globe that a flying saucer had been scooped up in Roswell, New Mexico, then swifly reported that the saucer wasn't a saucer at all, Roswell wrapped itself around the media. Through the early years, the single event of Roswell, even without a crumb of proof, augmented every image, word, and sound produced by the mass media. When it came time for people to make noise about Roswell, the town coveted the spotlight, placed there, naturally enough, through the mass media. In 1971, the *National Enquirer* held a contest—$5,000 to the reader who sent in the best UFO story. A few Roswell readers mailed in snippets of the '47 event, but alien abductions by then dominated the scene and Roswell couldn't compete with those tales. Then, in 1980, came *The Roswell Incident*, the book that launched a hundred-thousand lips. However, the real mass media push of Roswell arrived in 1989, via television, not surprisingly. In September of that year, *Unsolved Mysteries* produced a thirty-minute piece on the incident. Twenty-eight million people watched the show, and it reignited interest in the subject, brought out of the closet countless witnesses—or, more accurately, grandchildren of witnesses. Like a scuba diver's air bubbles, rumors rose to the surface.

Many people think that after 1947 Roswell the Incident suffered rigor mortis and slumped graveyard dead for three decades. Not so. After all, the initial story of the Roswell incident ("FLYING DISK RECOVERED" said a typical headline) appeared in more than 100 newspapers across the country, including *The New York Times*, and was heard on numerous radio bulletins. The story that something happened in southeast New Mexico never completely expired. Aided by what might be some military sleight-of-hand and alleged documented threats to keep quiet about that supposed juggling, the story merely lay fallow, napping in the collective subconscious as a dream, reappearing now and again over the years in various forms, thanks to the Pavlovian nature of popular culture.

The print media generally have been more restrained in their treatment of UFOs than have motion pictures and television, but the press has done its part to keep saucers in the limelight. The *National Enquirer* was the first publication to have a story about Roswell and what might have gone on there. The story ran in 1978 and included the first published interview with an eyewitness, former Roswell Army Air Field intelligence officer Jesse Marcel Sr., who had overseen the early retrieval of the debris. *Globe*, another tabloid, in 1981 broke a story that Oliver "Pappy" Henderson flew Roswell bodies to Wright Field, in Ohio. How did we know this? Because in the article Pappy's widow Sappho said he did.

One undeniable truth about the Roswell incident is that the principals have wonderful names: Pappy and Sappho; Lydia Sleppy, an Albuquerque radio station's teletype operator who in 1947 was going to transmit an "important story" before allegedy being cut off; Tess Truelove, the young woman with whom truck driver Jim Ragsdale said he was necking when the saucer slammed into a nearby hillside; Thaddeus Love, the soldier who reportedly accompanied the alien bodies to Fort Worth, Texas. Hollywood couldn't invent names like those. Even Mack Brazel, the laconic cowboy who stumbled onto what many calculated years later was the Roswell crashed saucer's detritus, is a fine, solid, live-off-the-land name, though the Brazel family has long given up trying to stop reporters from spelling it "Mac," instead of "Mack," the way it should.

If Roswell the Incident hovered about the periphery of American life, the news media overnight, it seemed, shoved the whole affair front and center: as it neared its fiftieth birthday, Roswell became a pop icon for UFOs in general. Major stories about possible military subterfuge in Roswell followed like marching soldiers: *Time, Popular Science,* a German magazine, a publication out of Turkey, the Sci-Fi channel, Israeli television. A good portion of one broadcast of *The NewsHour With Jim Lehrer* was devoted to debating the particulars of Roswell. Paul Harvey didn't know what to think of Roswell and its UFO, but when he plugged them both on his noontime radio show, up and down the Pecos Valley it was akin to hearing a papal blessing. No matter how you pronounced it, the city's name turned into a cultural codeword. Said UFO researcher Karl Pflock: "You mention Roswell on *Seinfeld,* and you don't even have to explain it." When the movie *Independence Day* came along in 1996, Roswell as an incident jumped right off the recognition chart. *Independence Day* not only reminded audiences that the event had occurred in 1947, but the movie suggested that Roswell stood for America's fight for freedom, liberty, and all things decent.

"Wuddent you a believer?" the Denny's waitress had asked. Whether I believe or don't believe is not the point here. Far more crucial is that all my life, without knowing it, I have been riding a great entertainment vehicle that Roswell gassed up. I am a child of Roswell, though I grew up 2,000 miles from New Mexico. As a kid, I had little interest in spacecraft or alien probes—until the mass media changed all that. When my father bought our family its first television set, a rhomboidal, zinc-tinted Admiral, in 1952, I vividly remember the first show I watched: *Captain Video and His Video Rangers.* More than anything in the world, I wanted to be a Junior Video Ranger. Dutifully, I sent away for Captain Video's secret decoder ring. When I received it, I found the ring didn't glow in the dark, as promised. Even so, I felt I had made a grand connection. Somehow, the ring would help me clean up this or that galaxy; the ring would make things right.

When I was about eight years old, Al Hodge, the actor who played Captain Video on TV, landed in a helicopter on the high school field in my Connecticut hometown. His appearance, heralded by my town's weekly newspaper, turned into the biggest event ever seen in the small community. It attracted several hundred kids, me among them. Captain Video was late arriving that day and we spectators were fretful that he might have been detained by—*Oh, no!*—the hideous Dr. Pauli. Then, finally, we heard the sound of a chopper. We looked up and shouted in rapture as the Captain, in military uniform, no less, hopped out and began to sign autographs. Prayers do get answered.

I didn't know it then, of course, but Captain Video had come indirectly from the plains north of *Rozzul*. When I was nine, I watched as television's *The Million Dollar Movie* broadcast *The Day the Earth Stood Still*, in one sense a Roswell refugee, every afternoon one week. I had trouble sleeping those nights as the ominous robot Gort clomped through my mind. When I was ten, my father picked up me and my brother, Tom, from a Little League baseball practice and took us to the first movie house we had ever been in. It was a warm June night in 1956 and I can still feel the air-conditioned chill of the Avon Theater. Better yet, I can still recall almost everything about that movie, *Forbidden Planet*, another stepchild of Roswell the Incident. Along with just about everybody else in the audience I laughed loudly when Robby the Robot whipped up enough bourbon to stock every wetbar in Las Vegas. And, like probably everyone around me, I felt the hairs on the back of my neck stand at attention when the awful invisible monster of *Forbidden Planet* approached the good guys' spaceship and squashed the steps of the craft as he silently climbed aboard.

Again, that monster was a being that had emerged, essentially, from the loins of Roswell. Twenty-five years later it led me to take my two sons to see their first movie, *E.T., The Extraterrestrial*, which in large measure Roswell also begat.

Susan Sontag said that most science-fiction monster films distract us and give us a false sense of security, just as most popular culture does. That's true. Deep down I surely knew there never could be an evil like the one in *Forbidden Planet*. But I still hoped, I still yearned. That turns out to be the same feeling expressed by most people who embrace Roswell. "If you don't believe," one disciple of Roswell the Incident advised me, "just pretend."

Those pulled along the path cleared by Roswell eventually were led to space travel. I was putting on my sneakers in gym class in 1961 when my junior high school's P.A. system relayed astronaut Alan Shepard's voice as he rose upward for his historic 15 minutes. *In a rocket!* If that one event helped to launch America's space efforts, it also helped to kick off America's fascination with space. The architect behind that fascination? Robert Hutchings Goddard who, during the 1930s and 1940s, lived and worked in Roswell the Place, profoundly motivated by the novels of H.G. Wells, a half-century before. Indeed, Goddard's vision of going to the moon caused me, when I was eleven years old, to "sign up" at New York City's Hayden Planetarium for a spaceship trip to that satellite. (On the sign-up sheet, I made sure to note that I wished to go on the "second" voyage to the moon.)

During the week I spent at Encounter '97, I watched hundreds of people walk down Roswell's Main Street and move merrily past the big rocket-launching tower that stands in front of the city's principal museum. Rarely did I see anyone stop to look at the tower. And yet the man responsible for that structure—Goddard—may have done more for Roswell the Incident than a dozen little gray men.

Although he may not have realized it, my father made me aware of how influential the creative process can be. A writer, Dad admired the work of science-fiction author Jack Williamson, and of journalist Walter Sullivan's 1964 landmark study of extraterrestrials, *We Are Not Alone*. Dad surely had heard of the Roswell incident; he had relatives in that corner of the Southwest. In 1960, he penned a screenplay titled *Take Me to Your Leader*, a sobering tale of six people who worry that one of them is an alien. Roswell reverberations: one of the characters claims to be a major in the U.S. Air Force Intelligence, sent to investigate whether a saucer has landed or if it is merely a weather balloon. The teleplay never got produced. However, it turned on a bulb in my brain, a light that showed me I didn't need to believe in something to believe that something happened. And that's really become the fundamental explanation of Roswell—that something happened there. That that something combined paranoia and the paranormal only intensified the illumination and the allure.

When the idea of flying saucers began to lift off in the late 1940s, the popular culture of flying saucers lifted off right with it. The late forties and early fifties were the years that made Roswell what it is today. Dig down and you'll find in that period the roots and the rise of UFOs. Like millions of other baby boomers, those also happened to be my growing up years.

Throughout the four decades that followed, UFOs were inseparably linked to the mass media's attention to two related and defining events of the post World War II period: the Cold War and cover-ups. For example, General Douglas MacArthur in a 1955 speech reported in *The New York Times*, shocked Americans silly when he said, "The nations of the world will have to unite, for the next war will be an interplanetary war. The nations of the earth must someday make a common front against atttack by people from other planets." A product of the Cold War, Roswell the Incident stood to remind us that the threat of hostility can be found everywhere. In other words, Roswell's very existence seemed to signal that if Soviet forces don't get us, then aliens from space probably will.

Visitor From a Small Planet, a Broadway play and then a Jerry Lewis movie in the late 1950s, kept UFOs on our mind, in particular the simmering scenario at Roswell. In the Gore Vidal play, when a character hears on the radio that a flying saucer may have landed, that news item and a follow-up mention of a likely cover-up so confuses him that he responds, "Venus is covered with ammonia and there's nothing but fungus on Mars. The Air Force is behind this. I knew it. I just knew it."

That something happened in Roswell, and that it had been cloaked, seems absolutely plausible today, for the landscape of New Mexico for years has involved military and governmental cover-ups of all kinds. Beginning with the decision in 1942 to develop an atomic bomb at Los Alamos, secrets large and small have been concealed across the state. Even the detonation of that bomb in 1945, in the desert a couple of hours from Roswell, was shielded from the public and blamed on the explosion of a weapons depot. At White Sands, a couple of hours from Roswell in another direction, destructive rockets regularly were test-launched, always far from prying eyes. At Holloman Air Force Base in Alamogordo, also close by, reconnaissance balloon flights took off for decades without the public knowing. The government consistently denied for ages the existence of a cache of nuclear weapons in the Manzano Mountains, near Albuquerque. Also near Albuquerque, in 1957 the Air Force mistakenly unloaded a hydrogen bomb, a 42,000-pound device 625 times more powerful than the one dropped on Hiroshima. Though no one was injured in the potentially catastrophic event, the military refused to let anyone know about it for almost thirty years.

During the 1950s my parents employed a live-in housekeeper, a sweet, elderly woman who resided in an attic bedroom of our Connecticut home. Late at night, while others slept, Priscilla would turn her scratchy radio to WOR in New York and the popular Long John Nebel Show. Lying in bed downstairs, I sometimes heard the voice of Nebel, who claimed he was from Venus, and of various guests who said they had flown to the studio that evening in a flying saucer, some from New Mexico. The Nebel show served as a forerunner to *Dreamland*, a 1990s, late-night, syndicated gabfest hosted by Art Bell, who has built a vast radio audience by reporting that pieces from the Roswell UFO crash definitely exist and that he owns one.

My mother and father would roll their eyes at breakfast when I told them about the latest Nebel program, but I kept listening, kept puzzling at the source of all this. I never was an obsessive fan of *Star Trek*, but I do know that its producers should regularly send a tithing to Roswell's Chamber of Commerce. As should the originators of *Alien*, as well as those people behind a freight of more recent TV series and films—from goose-bump-giving *Sliders* and *Millennium*, to such zany trifles as *Mars Attack!* and *My Stepmother Was an Alien*.

Anyone who thinks Americans in the sixties had other things to think about besides flying saucers need only take a look at *The New Yorker* magazine. In 1966 the publication bulged with humorous drawings about UFOs camouflaged by a Roswell-like Air Force, about "swamp gas" sightings and kidnappings by aliens, which had recently come into vogue largely through an experience reported by Betty and Barney Hill of Portsmouth, New Hampshire. *Look* magazine in the sixties serialized the Hills' story, from a book titled *The Uninterrupted Journey*, which then became a made-for-TV movie, *The UFO Incident*, starring James Earl Jones and Estelle Parsons. But the Hills surely grabbed more lasting fame by having their first names used by the creators of *The Flintstones*. Betty and Barney became the Rubbles—best friends to Fred and Wilma. In a memorable 1967 *Flintstones* comic book, extraterrestrials arrive in Bedrock to cause Fred Flintstone to shout, "Run, Barney, run! Them aliens mean business!" (Something happened there—and often it was funny.)

By 1969, the image of the flying saucer, piloted by a small humanoid extraterrestrial, was engraved in the nation's cerebrum. Approximately one in four Americans that year believed extraterrestrial beings had actually landed on Earth. Meanwhile, interest in Roswell percolated as UFO believers waited to find their Mecca. When they reached it, in the 1980s in southeast New Mexico, the worshipping commenced.

Social postulator John Fiske believes that popular culture tends to be excessive, that its brush strokes are broad, its colors bright. Indeed, Roswell's canvas includes everything from the lines of dialogue in a screenplay, to the punchline of a joke heard in fifty states. Roswell may have its little gray men, but the town's palette brightens considerably each July with the appearance of piles of little green paper.

The remains of Roswell rest everywhere, for popular culture tends to not miss any form of pleasure. Roswell is scattered through dusty archives of libraries, and on the sides of spanking-new U-Haul trucks. It pops out of the pages of beach novels, and it clings to the marquees of movie theaters, blinking in neon for all to see, to nod at, to be mortified by, to laugh about, to sigh over, to make us believe even more.

As my father might have put it, Roswell is our punishment. But it's also our prize.

chapter 1

A Touchstone for Our Times

"Roswell! You know us as a UFO town, but there's so much more!"
— *U.S. News & World Report*, 1997

MOST STAUNCH BELIEVERS SAY that a U.S. Army Air Corps flatbed truck rumbled down Main Street in Roswell, New Mexico, the night of July 4, 1947, or maybe July 5. In the back of that truck, beneath a tarpulin, most believers say, was a spaceship and the bodies of three aliens, or maybe four.

Hinkel's, a popular Roswell department store, in the summer of 1947 was holding its annual July 4th sale—Manhattan dress shirts were priced from fifty cents to five dollars. Down the block, Zinks was selling vacuum cleaners for $59.95. Sears, Roebuck & Co. of Roswell had a sectional sofa marked down to $149, and a dinette set going for $69.99. You could smell the sharp leather from Edd Amonett's Saddle Shop on Main Street, just as you could get a sweet whiff from nearby Kipling's Fountain. If you switched on the radio that weekend in Roswell, to KGLF, you might hear *Lum 'n' Abner*. If you opened the *Roswell Daily Record*, you could turn to the comics and catch up on *Little Orphan Annie* or *Moon Mullins*.

If, as most believers say it did, the flatbed truck bounced along Main toward the Roswell Army Air Field, it sped directly past Kessel's

Department Store, City Drug, Jinks Graham's Central Barber Shop, Frankie Sargent's bar and pool hall, Hugh Huff's jewelry shop, and the Plains Theater, now home of the International UFO Museum and Research Center. On July 4, 1947, the Plains advertised itself as "cool," for Roswell any year can be truly blistering during the summer. Tickets cost ten and fifty cents, depending on where you sat, and *Boomerang* had just opened at the Plains for two nights. Good cast: Dana Andrews, Jane Wyatt, Arthur Kennedy, Lee J. Cobb. Good director: a fledgling Elia Kazan. Good picture: a noirish, cleanly made crime film, based on a true story of a prosecutor who finds the accused is innocent. "Suspense that turns your heart into a hammerbeat," said the ad in the *Daily Record*.

Good grief: the coincidence is too much to overlook. A boomerang happens to be a type of UFO, the kind that pilot Kenneth Arnold, who recorded the first saucer sighting in the nation on June 24, 1947, in Washington state, said the flying disks resembled. They were V-shaped, Arnold recollected, and all were similar to a boomerang. Coincidence—real or imagined—has come to play a large and important role in ufology, so large that a law, the Coincidental Corollary exists solely to encompass that role. The Coincidental Corollary says that if something happened once, it will happen again, much like before, even if it never really happened the first time. For instance, the little gray men seen at Roswell now populate most accounts of space aliens everywhere. Of the thousands of UFOs spotted in the last few decades, most look very much like the boomerangish one that was said to have plowed into a hill northwest of Roswell.

They're still spotted, these boomerangs, mostly at night. Some boomerangs have been reported to be as large as a football field. Most though, are comparatively small, perhaps twenty-five feet, tip to tip. UFO skeptics, however, say a bunch of boomerangs are usually nothing more than a flock of migrating birds.

Roswell had 25,000 people in July 1947. Few outsiders paid much attention to the community, even though it was a county seat, a gathering place for cowboys, a military town. All of that was before UFO devotees started showing up. Nearly 50,000 people live there now. There's a history to the place, and that history is key to understanding why so many UFO enthusiasts come to Roswell each summer. Which is to say this: not everything is what you think it is.

For instance, a marker in Roswell salutes the town's first distinguished citizen—John Simpson Chisum. He was one of the biggest landholders in the country, one of the wealthiest cattlemen anywhere. To call him a hero, however, would be nonsensical. Chisum, not to be confused with Jesse Chisolm, who opened the first cattle trail to Kansas, was born in Tennessee in 1824. As a young man, Chisum drove a herd of cattle to Kansas, but the task drove him to bankruptcy. To get out of that jam, he claimed his only assets were Texas livestock, which he didn't own. Simply, Chisum lied.

When he settled in Texas, Chisum bought a slave girl to be his cook and housekeeper and she later became his lover and bore him two daughters. But Chisum, who never married, deserted the three to relocate elsewhere in Texas. A relative had told Chisum about the good money that could be made in the New Mexico Territory. The relative also told Chisum that he had killed a man in New Mexico, a fact that seemed far less interesting to Chisum. Stirred by the prospect of financial gain, Chisum in 1867 drove a herd of 600 beef cattle out of Texas, following the historic path blazed by two other prominent Texans, Charles Goodnight and Oliver Loving. Chisum led his cattle close by what is now Roswell. When he reached the Bosque Redondo, near Fort Sumner, Chisum quickly sold his stock. The buyer was the government, which needed the beef to feed 7,000 Navajo men, women, and children who had been uprooted from their homes in the Arizona Territory and forced to march to Fort Sumner, where they were imprisoned.

Like the relative's admission of murder, the Indians' deplorable situation apparently didn't bother Chisum, for he immediately filled another order, and agreed to bring more than 10,000 cattle to

Bosque Redondo. In truth, Chisum had little regard for Indians. If they happened to get in his way, he had someone shoot them. "Big Hat," the Indians called Chisum for his ten-gallon chapeau. A self-serving opportunist who lusted for power, wealth, and prestige, a man who could be ornery as a badger, Chisum feared no one. Even when Billy the Kid, New Mexico's most famous outlaw, announced he was going to gun down Chisum for allegedly not paying the Kid for protecting his range in the celebrated and bloody Lincoln County War, Chisum didn't flinch.

As Chisum's herds grew, to keep track of his many cattle he branded them with his own special signature. This was no little nick but rather a slash—called the "Long Rail" brand—that ran behind the animal's left shoulder in one straight line hindward across the ribs. The garish carving alone didn't satisfy Chisum. He desired a second marking, a deeper, more prominent one— on the ears. He made it by sticking a knife through the bottom part of a critter's ear, near the root, and slicing upward, almost halfway. This left part of the ear standing upright, with maybe two-thirds of it dropping down to bounce about. "Maybe them derned ears won't jingle," Chisum said with a deep laugh, "but they sure as heck will bob." The "Jinglebob" brand, cowboys called the grotesque mutilation, and it gained great notoriety throughout the Southwest. Roswell eventually became known as the Jinglebob Town and even today most old-time range riders would rather talk about that crazy brand than about that crazy UFO. There was nothing a cattle rustler could do when he came upon, say, a cow with a jinglebob cut, which made the cow appear as if it had four ears instead of two. There was nothing to do except hack off the animal's ears altogether, which some rustlers actually did.

Cancer finally claimed the Cattle King of New Mexico in 1884 at age sixty. By then Chisum had settled in South Spring Ranch, seven miles below Roswell. He left Roswell with a dusty, toothpick-chewin', cattle-carvin', weather-talkin' legacy. (A six-inch rainfall area ranchers like to say, is one drop every six inches). Chisum also left behind a fancy house filled with black servants.

Blacks in Roswell never had it easy, a notion that Frank Boyer found out in 1908. In search of freedom, Boyer had walked to the New Mexico Territory that year from his native Georgia. He and his wife, Ella, had wanted to live in Roswell, but they found the town fiercely segregated so they set down roots about nine miles south of where the Army Air Field later stood. There the Boyers and a few other friends homesteaded in a place they called Blackdom. They built a school, a church, post office, general store, some modest homes, and attempted to eke out a living by raising chickens, hogs, and grain sorghum. Residents of Blackdom held ice cream socials at the church, fielded a good baseball team, and every June 19 celebrated Juneteenth, in observation of the emancipation of Texas slaves in 1865. At one point the settlement had 300 people and spanned 15,000 acres.

Blackdom residents didn't have much to do with Roswell for they didn't feel welcome there. If a black man tried to hitchhike to Roswell, he'd likely find it impossible to get a ride. In time, blacks did move to town, where they organized their own school, called Carver School, but it never was formally recognized by whites as an educational institution.

Droughts and discouragement eventually wiped away Blackdom in the mid-1920s, and the townsite virtually disappeared. Today, Blackdom is a barren patch of land that is scarcely commemorated by any local historical group. Even with Blackdom gone, segregation and racism remained fixtures in the community. The Roswell Chamber of Commerce told the WPA Guide to New Mexico in the 1930s that no blacks lived in Roswell when, in fact, dozens did. As recently as the early 1950s a sign in the window of a popular Roswell café said, "NIGGERS AND DOGS EAT AROUND BACK." An incident in 1952 helped to set the stage for racial change in Roswell.

On a cool November night that year, the Albuquerque High School Bulldogs arrived in town for a football game with the Roswell High School *Ky-oats*. The two teams, once rivals, hadn't met in six years. In 1947, Albuquerque High was headed for a game at Roswell when school officials in that city gave Albuquerque High administrators this warning: Don't bring your Negro football players down here. Angered, Albuquerque Public Schools superintendent John Milne canceled the game and, ultimately, the series. By 1952, racial tensions had eased enough for Albuquerque High School to put Roswell back on its schedule.

Roswell had no blacks on its 1952 football team, while Albuquerque had a handful, including a rangy wide receiver. Velma Corley had just joined the squad, a junior so green he didn't know how to put on his shoulder pads. Corley got to make the trip to Roswell because the starter at offensive end, Jack Holstein, had been injured.

That night was homecoming and a large crowd watched as Roswell led 6–0 for most of the game. In the final minute, Albuquerque High scored on a safety to make the game 6–2. Then, with just seconds remaining, the Albuquerque quarterback threw a desperation pass. A Roswell defender deflected the ball and it sailed downfield into the arms of an alert Vel Corley, who raced into the end zone untouched as the gun sounded. The final score: Albuquerque 8, Roswell 6. Many people, the press included, believed that Holstein had scored the touchdown, for Corley had been given Holstein's jersey. When word got out who the star of the game was, the irony was lost on no one.

Today, blacks make up about five percent of Roswell, and they play an even smaller role in the town's UFO activities. Indeed, blacks and outer space seldom have found a comfortable partnership. Major Robert Lawrence Jr., an Air Force pilot, was killed during a training exercise in 1967, six months after he was named to the Air Force's manned orbiting laboratory program, then a separate entity from NASA. Sadly, it took thirty years after his death for Lawrence to be recognized as a full-fledged astronaut, the first black astronaut. If blacks do get involved with UFOs, it almost seems surprising. For instance, when thirty-nine members of the Heaven's Gate cult killed themselves in 1997 while waiting to rendezvous with an alien spaceship that they believed was coming to Earth via the Hale-Bopp comet, the mass suicide didn't stun some observers as much as the death of a single member. Thomas Alva Nichols, fifty-nine, an Arizona resident, was black. More important to UFO buffs and Roswell aficionados was that Nichols was the brother of Nichelle Nichols, the actress who played Lieutenant Uhuru, the communications officer aboard *The Enterprise*, on the original *Star Trek* television series.

It is a rare sight to see a black visiting either of Roswell's two UFO museums. And of the thousands of people who came to Roswell for a week in July 1997, black visitors could be counted on one hand. It's not a case of blacks feeling unwanted; rather, it's as if blacks have enough problems getting along in this world without worrying about other worlds.

And yet the race-charged John Sayles's film *The Brother From Another Planet* (1984), is one of the most sharp-witted extraterrestrial movies made. A black alien escapes from slavery on another planet, splashes down in New York's Hudson River, staggers up to Harlem where he hangs out in a saloon. Seemingly a comedy, *The Brother From Another Planet* makes some powerful statements about a person's skin color:

"Where you from, brother?" a barfly asks.

The alien visitor points a thumb skyward.

"Uptown? South Bronx?"

Blacks have not been the only group in Roswell to take their lumps. When word came that Roswell was getting a military base in August 1941, the city cheered wildly and lined up for a parade. The new base at first was called the Roswell Army Flying School and was really just rows of tents. As the war escalated, however, the installation grew and in 1942 the base became the Roswell

23

Army Air Field. By 1945, 14,000 students, including pilots, co-pilots, bombardiers and flight engineers trained in four-engine planes there. B-17s, B-36s, B-52s dotted the tarmacs. The elite 509th Composite Group that had unloaded atomic bombs on Japan came to Roswell and the Enola Gay occupied a spot on the runway. For a time, the place became known as Roswell Air Field, when the Air Force broke with the Army in the fall of 1947. Then, in January 1948, the field was designated a permanent base and named Walker Air Force Base, in honor of General Kenneth N. Walker, of Cerrillos, New Mexico, who had perished in the Pacific Theater in 1942. K-135 and B-52 pilots trained at Roswell, as Walker became part of the Strategic Air Command, or SAC. The grounds swelled to 800 buildings. In 1960, Walker was designated a support base for a squadron of Atlas Intercontinental missiles. But almost as quickly as the missile sites were built around Roswell, they were dismantled. In March 1965, the Air Force announced the deactivation of the missile squadron and 3,000 people were affected. Things moved quickly after this, for the United States military had work to do in Southeast Asia, moreso than in Russia or Cuba. In December 1965, the Department of Defense began making burial plans for Walker. By 1967, the base was gone.

The closing of Walker shocked Roswell, for no one in the city truly believed it would happen. Few were prepared as the town's major cash flow suddenly began to dry up. The economy plunged: stores closed, businesses moved, and residents fled as a shabby, boarded-up appearance took over. The spiffy Roswell Inn, opened in 1961, looked ancient only a decade later. It took almost fifteen years for Roswell to recover. Opening the wound further, Dr. David Reuben, a psychiatrist at Walker Air Force Base from 1959–1961, went on television often in the late 1960s and early 1970s, to promote his book *Everything You Always Wanted To Know About Sex (But Were Afraid to Ask)*. Again and again Reuben would joke with Johnny Carson on *The Tonight Show* about men Reuben knew in the Air Force who had foot fetishes or who liked to have sexual intercourse with farm animals. Reuben's book later became a Woody Allen movie, though most people with a Walker background did not laugh much at that either.

By the late 1970s, Roswell had begun to turn itself around, especially after the base became the Roswell Industrial Air Center, its name today. But there have been problems there, too. A bus manufacturer, housed in an old B-36 hangar, came and went and came again, periodically causing traumatic layoffs among the city's workforce. Additional businesses such as the nation's largest mozzarella plant, and an outfit that makes lollipops have boosted Roswell's economy, though at the same time brought snickers. In 1996, when David Letterman dispatched a glassy-eyed flake named Manny the Hippie to do street reporting as he traveled across the country, producers organized a stop in Roswell to check out UFOs. The Letterman skit on the *The Late Show*, in which Manny searched for residents with antennae, further led the nation to believe that Roswell was a different kind of place. (Manny the Hippie's fame lasted far less longer than Roswell's: law enforcement authorities recognized him on TV as a parole violator and abruptly ended his reporting career.)

Chisum's bloody bravado, racial strife, and the folding of the Air Force base, gave Roswell an inferiority complex. What's more, Roswell, people knew, wasn't really a tourist town. It offered few real attractions and it possessed a worrisome crime rate. That's why when Roswell officials suggested reaching out for UFOs, most townspeople rushed up to grab. Something positive had finally happened in Roswell, something good had finally occurred, even if it was a mite strange.

To understand the growing power of UFOs, all one need do is realize that two events occurring on the same date as the Roswell incident have been virtually swept aside. In terms of American culture, these two other events should rightfully hold eminent positions. However, they've been nearly eradicated by a nation's fixation with flying saucers.

On July 3, 1947, Bill Veeck, the ebullient owner of the Cleveland Indians baseball team, bought the contract of Larry Doby from the Newark Eagles of the Negro League. Eleven weeks earlier, Jackie Robinson had become the first black Major League Baseball player when he played in a game with the Brooklyn Dodgers. Robinson's entrance into baseball changed the nature of the game forever and the course of race in this country.

But now the American League needed a black player and Veeck decided on Larry Doby, a gifted, all-around athlete from Paterson, New Jersey. On July 5, 1947—the day when legions of Roswell UFO followers are certain a crashed spaceship was being retrieved northwest of Roswell—Doby pinch-hit in a game against the Chicago White Sox. He struck out, then played first base in the second game of a doubleheader, and drove in a run. Quiet and polite like Robinson, Doby didn't start again the rest of the year. He wound up batting a lowly .156 in 29 games, a humble beginning for what turned out to be a fine career.

On July 4, 1947, a rowdy motorcyle gang called the Boozefighters, one of the first biker clubs in the nation, took to the road in search of adventure. From south-central Los Angeles, the black-leather wearing group arrived in the small northern California farm town of Hollister. The gang was led by "Wino Willie" Forkner, who had earned his nickname at age twelve for chugging red wine. The Boozefighters were among about 4,000 bikers attending a rally that weekend, eighty-five miles southeast of San Francisco. The bikers rode through bars, got drunk, and left broken beer bottles everywhere. Dozens were arrested for drunkenness and reckless driving. A group led by Forkner marched to Hollister's city jail and demanded their friends be released. Subsequently a riot broke out—the Battle of Hollister, it's been termed. Forkner was arrested, and spent the night behind bars.

A photograph of the ruckus in *Life* magazine gave the American public its first look at the menacing image of bikers. Six years later, that image led to the creation of the Hollywood movie *The Wild One*, starring Marlon Brando, in only his fifth movie. The film turned into a cult classic and became the first major movie to confront the seismic rift that opened between generations in the fifties. Brando, in a black leather jacket, white T-shirt, jeans, motorcycle hat and sunglasses, became a voice for an entire generation. Suddenly, black leather jackets, white T-shirts, and jeans grew into symbols of rebellion. "Juvenile delinquency" became an overnight phrase. Senate hearings and best-sellers on the subject followed, gangs formed around the world, and in 1965 a hit song appeared by the Shangri-Las, *Leader of the Pack* (It came complete with the sound of squealing tires and breaking glass). Today, *The Wild One* is most noted for two lines of dialogue: "Hey, Johnny," asks a teen-aged girl in town of the Brando character, "what are you rebelling against?" Astride his monstrous Harley-Davidson, Brando cocks his head and answers with a sneer, "Whaddya got?"

It would be safe to say that far fewer people in this country have heard of Larry Doby and Wino Willie Forkner than have heard of Roswell, New Mexico. But that's the trendy nature of popular culture. Doby too often gets unfairly labeled as a follower: second to Jackie Robinson on a whites-only baseball field. Doby also was the second man, after Frank Robinson, to become a major league manager. But Doby achieved more than footnote status. He and the much better known Satchel Paige were the first blacks to play in the World Series, in 1948. Doby, in fact, won Game Four of that Series with a home run. In 1954, Doby became the first black player to hit a home run in an All-Star game. He finished his thirteen-year career in 1959.

More significantly, when Doby began in the major leagues he had to endure the same sort of treatment that Jackie Robinson did. Teammates shunned him in the beginning, he could not eat in certain restaurants or stay in selected hotels on road trips. Through it all, Doby, as Robinson had done, didn't complain or fight back;

he turned the other cheek. In 1996, former National League president Bill White said this of Doby, who still works in Major League Baseball as an administrator: "One of the great pioneers of our society, who also happened to be a great ballplayer." Baseball's Hall of Fame at Cooperstown, New York, enshrined Doby in 1998.

Through the years, Wino Willie Forkner would return to Hollister for celebrations, where he often autographed jackets and T-shirts. Oddly, Forkner disliked *The Wild One* because he thought the image Brando portrayed was exaggerated. Forkner had plans to attend the fiftieth anniversary of the Hollister rally. "Going to Hollister is what is keeping me alive," he told friends in 1997. He had hoped to lead motorcyclists through the streets there and a large crowd, though not nearly the size as the one expected to descend on Roswell for the party marking the fiftieth year since the alleged UFO incident, was anticipated. Forkner never made it back to Hollister. He died June 23, 1997, of a ruptured aortic aneurysm, in Santa Rosa, California. He was seventy-six.

Frank Joyce didn't make it back to Roswell, either. In July 1947, Joyce worked as an announcer/reporter for Roswell radio station KGFL. He had interviewed by telephone Mack Brazel shortly after Brazel discovered debris from a suspected saucer, and Joyce suggested Brazel tell authorities at Roswell Army Air Field. Joyce was the first person to be given the celebrated RAAF press release, in 1947. He subsequently wired the story of that release to United Press, after which he received a threatening phone call from someone who identified himself as a Pentagon official. Joyce later met with Brazel, who by then had reportedly changed his original story. "You know how some folks talk about little green men?" Brazel said. "Well, they ain't green." They were gray, of course.

Frank Joyce grew up in Roswell, and for many years he didn't talk about a spaceship setting down north of town. He was afraid to. When the story finally broke and became known around the world, Joyce didn't like it. He is mentioned in most accounts of the Roswell incident and is portrayed in the Showtime cable network movie *Roswell*. But Joyce said the incident has brought him more headaches than anything else. For instance, a next-door neighbor in Albuquerque, amused by Joyce's connection to Roswell's most famous event, used to sneak up to Joyce's bedroom window late at night and make *Twilight Zone* noises—*Deedeedeedee, deedeedeedee*. After a long career as a newsman with KOB-TV in Albuquerque, Joyce is now retired. Ruddy-faced and white-haired, he seldom returns to Roswell and made it a point to not attend the Encounter '97 festivities. "All those nuts dressed up with propellers on their heads, it's a mockery," he says.

According to Joyce, strange things were happening in Roswell long before 1947. "There used to be caves west of town, along a ridgeline out there. Kids were always getting lost in there and at least one boy never came out. One day I went there with some Boy Scouts. We went to a place they called Forbidden Cave. It was a hole that dropped straight down and sulphur fumes were coming out of it. Anyway, we made a ladder and went down in. What I saw scares the daylights out of me to this day. Sitting on a ledge in that cave were two alligator-like things. Four feet long each. These weren't Gila monsters. They were much, much bigger. I climbed right back up that ladder quick as I could. The city fathers finally went in and dynamited the caves. Closed them up."

Roswell's Bottomless Lake State Park also intrigued Joyce. Named by cowboys who once tied lariats together, dropped a plumb line down, and decided the pools were never-ending, the lakes actually are sinkholes, some at least ninety feet deep. "Cars were always dropping in there," says Joyce, "never to be found again."

What then of the flying saucer that supposedly crashed? "I was there when it happened and I've read so much about it," says Joyce, "but damned if I know what's true anymore. I'll tell you one thing, though. The only place where that thing coulda happened was the place where people said it happened. In Roswell."

Just as exploring Forbidden Cave didn't cause Roswell to completely disappear, sighting a UFO didn't, by itself, spring Roswell to enduring fame. Indeed, it is clear now that the history of rocketry and the conquest of space, two eras that sandwiched the events of the summer of 1947, contributed greatly to the city's illustriousness.

chapter 2

This Man Had a Real Blast

"I'd like to say 'Hi' to my granddaddy in Roswell, New Mexico."
—Martian addressing Pathfinder rover, *New Yorker* cartoon, 1997

OMITTING THE NAME ROBERT GODDARD from a list of Roswell's UFO personalities is a bit like leaving Tang off an inventory of outer space beverages. And yet such an oversight typically happens to Goddard. After all, as the father of modern rocketry, Robert Hutchings Goddard had nothing to do with flying saucers; he died two years before the Roswell incident. Lord knows what he would have made of "(Jim) Beam Me Up" on the side of shot glasses marketed in Roswell, or "Probe This" on the front of sweatshirts for sale in the city.

Goddard did, however, understand that space travel could be possible, and he labored to make it as acceptable as bus travel. Which helps to explain why so many people have faith in things extraterrestrial, and why those same people are cocksure a UFO could make scheduled stops throughout the universe. What's more, Goddard worked to set the mold for the American astronaut, who became a holy man of popular culture. The very nature of the astronaut gives good weight to a belief in the Something's-Out-There philosophy. After all: why else would anyone bother going out there?

So, in a tangential way, Goddard may have had more to do with what happened in Roswell than anyone else.

That Goddard is remembered in Roswell is somewhat surprising, for Roswell has not always treated its heroes well. Not its celebrities, not such stars as actress Demi Moore, or the late singer John Denver, who each took their first breaths in the town and are hailed as if they had lived there for eons when in actuality neither remained much longer than it takes to be born. And though the late cowboy actor/singer Roy Rogers stayed only long enough in Roswell in 1933 to eat a pie and get married, he is considered by some to be a native. Rogers was Leonard Slye in those pre-Dale Evans days, and when he performed in Roswell with a visiting band over KGFL, Arlene Wilkins, a female listener, came by the radio station with a plate of food in her hands and a sparkle in her eyes. She soon became Rogers's first wife.

On the other hand, Bob Crosby, a calf and steer roping standout, a rodeo cowboy many swear was the best to ever fork a saddle, spent twenty-five years or so in the community. However, for a long time Roswell tried to forget him. Crosby had a reputation as a gritty competitor who snarled back at pain; it was said that he had broken every bone in his body at least once. To one of his severely damaged legs he once applied his own cast, a poultice made mostly of cow manure. The maggots, Crosby figured, would eat the rotting flesh and cleanse the area. Crosby was even rougher on his rodeo horses—he overtrained them, beat them, even bit them.

Though he lived with his family in town, in a house on Riverside Drive, Bob Crosby also maintained a ranch near Kenna, New Mexico, northeast of Roswell. In 1947, three months after the Roswell incident, Crosby, headed for his ranch. Alone in his Jeep, he veered off the road and plowed nose first into an arroyo. He suffered massive head injuries and was dead at age fifty.

Crosby's grave is well-marked at Roswell's South Park Cemetery, but for decades the town did little to mark his achievements. Irascible and egotistical, he apparently made along the way a slew of enemies. In 1993, Crosby's hometown finally got around to saluting him by dedicating the Bob Crosby Arena at the Eastern New Mexico Fairgrounds.

Professional golf star Nancy Lopez underwent similar treatment. Lopez grew up in Roswell and learned to play golf there, tutored by her father, Domingo, a sweet-tempered former migrant laborer who worked as an auto-body repairman. Domingo, fondly called "Sunday," had learned golf in his middle-age by sneaking onto Roswell courses. When he started teaching Nancy, and saw that she was a natural, he built a sandtrap in the family's small, east-side backyard. Nancy Lopez became a child prodigy. When she was eleven, she nearly won the state women's amateur championship. She did win it the next three years as well as several significant junior titles around the country. As outstanding as Nancy Lopez became in golf, however, Roswell seemed reluctant to hold her dear. The local country club, which had the best course in town, never offered the Lopezes' a membership, playing privileges, or much support, even when the Lopezes', hardly wealthy people, desperately needed assistance for Nancy to improve. Reasons for the snub weren't explained, but eventually it became clear: the Lopezes' were Hispanic, Domingo had once picked cotton for a living, and the family lived in *La Gara*, or "the rag" section, a poor Roswell neighborhood named for those who hung their tattered laundry outdoors.

Girls were not allowed to compete in organized athletics in New Mexico when Nancy Lopez started high school in Roswell in the early 1970s, so she tried out for the boys's golf team. She met such resistance the family eventually took the matter to court and won a landmark case. Ultimately, Nancy led her high school boys' golf team to a state championship.

After she turned professional, Lopez went on to win almost fifty tournaments and the Ladies Professional Golf Association enshrined her in its Hall of Fame. Early in her pro career, Lopez had decided that she no longer wanted to make her home in Roswell. "Too many bad memories," she told friends. Surely embarrassed by the schism, in 1991 Roswell embraced her. Sensing the potential of a UFO windfall, the town had begun to promote its all-American image to vacationers. Nancy Lopez, it was decided, should be part of that image and so the Flora Vista Elementary School, which Lopez had attended as a girl, was renamed in her honor.

Like Bob Crosby and Nancy Lopez, Robert Goddard was not born in Roswell. Nonetheless, most of his rocketry experiments were done in Roswell, not far from the road that leads to where many people are positive a UFO crash-landed.

Goddard wasn't around for the advent of extraterrestrials, but his fertilization of the space program brought closer to home the idea of a busy galaxy, one which well could include restless aliens. There probably would be UFOs sightings without the help of Robert Goddard, but there wouldn't be an emphasis on space as a reachable destination without him. And there likely wouldn't be a shelf of best-selling books and a wealth of well-attended movies, nor would television sets across the land be worn down from broadcasting one space mission after another if it weren't for Robert Hutchings Goddard.

Born October 5, 1882 in Worcester, Massachusetts, Goddard himself was a part of the very early years of pop culture when, as a boy he picked up H.G. Wells's classic novel *The War of the Worlds*, published in 1898, and then read and reread the famed opening sentence: "No one would have believed . . . . " Wells's description of Martians, somehow safely landing after a journey of roughly 140,000,000 miles, stuck in young Goddard's mind like a favorite tune.

The bellicose Martians, as Wells pictured them, were frightening, polyp-like blobs of brain matter, equipped with astonishing mechanisms for movement and battle. Goddard was sixteen when he read that, and the words stirred him and set into motion his life's challenge—to reach the Red Planet, a place that did *not* have a candy bar named after it. Goddard reinforced that inner drive by inhaling newspaper serials of the day, features such as Jules Verne's *From the Earth to the Moon*, Joseph Atterlay's *A Voyage to the Moon*, and Garrett P. Serviss's *Edison's Conquest of Mars*. But it was Wells's vivid imagination that truly fixed Goddard's gaze upward. Years later, Goddard wrote Wells a letter saying that *The War of the Worlds* cast a spell over him as a boy, and continued to move him as a man. He added in his letter a happy birthday greeting to Wells. "Thank you," Wells tersely wrote back, obviously preoccupied with other matters.

Goddard's parents encouraged their only child's curiosity. His father, Nahum, a traveling salesman, was a tinkerer, an inventor who created, among other things, a knife to skin rabbits. Young Goddard—called Robbie in those days—was a sickly boy who found comfort in books. At the public library in Boston he memorized chunks of material on electricity, chemistry, crystals, and the atmosphere. Any account of space travel struck him, including reports of the celebrated "Moon Hoax" of 1853. The tale originated in a series of newspaper articles in *The New York Sun* written by an overly ambitious journalist named Richard Locke. The stories told of Sir John Herschel, a famous astronomer who had devised the most powerful telescope ever made. Herschel's creation could see astonishing things—strange plants, animals, and flying creatures, all obviously intelligent and all—on the surface of the moon! Sales of the *Sun,* already the largest circulating newspaper in the world, skyrocketed even more until another reporter exposed Locke and caused him to admit he had fabricated the articles. The "Moon Hoax" today stands as the first clear case of skeptical debunking. Though the story occurred almost 100 years before the Roswell incident, it showed Goddard how hungry, how ready people were even then to accept life on other planets.

Not simply satisfied with reading the books, Goddard, trying to decide what could be true and what might never be, scribbled notes in the margins of pages. When he perused Wells's *Fighters From Mars*, for instance, Goddard grew excited to think of alien invaders marching down the streets of Boston. *But how would they get there?* he jotted beside the text.

In time, Goddard went from exigeses to experiments—at first merely with balloons and hydrogen. Soon he decided that traveling in space and going beyond the pull of Earth's gravity might be accomplished if someone were to invent a super-powerful rocket.

As a teenager, Goddard developed what would later be diagnosed as tuberculosis. Seeking a better climate for their son, his parents left Boston to resettle near relatives in Worcester. To build himself up, as well as to seek answers about his future, Goddard began to take long walks alone around Worcester. On one stroll in late 1899, Goddard stopped at a wispy cherry tree on his Aunt Effie's strawberry farm. He studied the tree for a moment, then climbed it and scooted along a branch, where he sat fixed. At age seventeen, perched in a tree with the stars to keep him company, Goddard decided once and for all to devote himself to space travel. It was an unknown field then, laughed at by many. But on that night and in that tree, Goddard was determined to play a role. Words of Jules Verne ran through his mind: "If you can see it, you can do it." This is what he saw: a machine that would travel to the planets, even though airplane travel hadn't even been achieved.

By 1903, when the Wright Brothers flew their first plane, Goddard was already visualizing space flight. He went on to Clark University in Worcester where he studied physics and engineering and where he later became a full professor. In addition to his academic duties, Goddard continued to conduct experiments, now at Aunt Effie's farm, where he stored his equipment in a henhouse. During World War I he developed bazooka rockets for the U.S. Army to use to stop German tanks. But his real goal was not to send an object on a horizontal path, but to launch it vertically, and on March 16, 1926, he fired the first successful liquid-fueled rocket. Though Goddard's creation traveled only forty-one feet, held back by a shortage of money, it was an event as significant as the first manned flight.

Few people in those days understood Goddard's genius. Outwardly he seemed just a strange little stooped fellow with a bald head, sunken chest, and guarded manner. When Goddard talked of the "infinite altitude" of a rocket, the words brought him the same sort of derision that came when some Roswell residents years later first mentioned a flying saucer. Not long after Goddard published his astonishing pamphlet *A Method of Reaching Extreme Altitudes*, in 1919, which talked of firing rockets to the moon, he became the "Moon Man" to the media and he was repeatedly asked for free tickets to the next rocket ship going there. The *Boston American* even labeled him a "mad scientist." Everybody chuckled, it seemed, except for German rocket scientist Hermann Oberth, who wrote Goddard as early as 1922 to ask for launch tips, and the Weather Bureau, which asked Goddard's opinion of using rockets to collect high-altitude information that would make forecasting more reliable.

So there he was, Robbie Goddard, traipsing over his aunt's strawberry plants, setting off his homemade rockets, and paying little attention to what anybody thought. However, toward the end of the 1920s, the area fire marshal apparently had enough of the "Moon Man." After one tremendously loud and fiery explosion, Goddard was banned from any more experiments lest he burn down neighboring barns and scorch the surrounding countryside.

In truth, the ban did not disappoint Goddard, for he knew he needed a clear, uninhabited place to set off his rockets, a high-altitude plain where he wouldn't alarm the citizenry. He also desired a climate that would soothe his troubled lungs. After some checking, Goddard came up with Roswell, New Mexico. Though Goddard's tuberculosis had been arrested, it still bothered him on occasion. Roswell, like some other Southwestern locales, was receptive to TB health-seekers, and even recruited them.

Thus, in 1930, Goddard and his wife, Esther, who had no children, motored West in a red, second-hand Packard coupe. When they arrived in southeast New Mexico, the couple immediately knew they had found the perfect spot. Roswell in the thirties was a small, well-appointed town surrounded by open prairie. With cloudless skies much of the time, and a high elevation, the area invited flight. Indeed, the isolation of the entire state of New Mexico proved attractive. Within a decade of Goddard's arrival, all sorts of people—from atomic scientists at Los Alamos, to technicians at the Army's rocket proving grounds at White Sands, descended upon New Mexico.

Though it had only 11,000 people, Roswell and its environs in 1930 possessed a rich and colorful past. Billy the Kid, about whom more would be eventually written than even the Roswell incident, had lived in the area. The Kid was buried to the north, at Fort Sumner, though, like Roswell's flying saucer history, some doubted that fact. The Goddards bought a house on the north edge of Roswell, on Mescalero Road, and Robert was given use of 16,000 acres north of there, on a flat, bone-dry stretch called Eden Valley. Here, among scorpions and wild rabbits, Goddard and a team of workers he had brought with him from Massachusetts set up a launching tower. Goddard's goal was to build a more powerful, lightweight rocket motor capable of withstanding the high temperatures generated in the combustion chambers. Additionally, Goddard planned to work on gyroscopic stabilization systems so that his rocket would not veer off course. And, he wanted to rig his rocket to a parachute so he could use it again and again.

"The Professor," Roswell people began to call the man in the floppy hat who seldom left the Mescalero ranch. To strangers, The Professor sometimes showed a crooked smile beneath his moustache, but he seemed terribly private, even to the German scientists who continued to beseech him for information.

Goddard fired his first liquid-propelled rocket in Roswell on December 30, 1930, and it reached 2,000 feet. Two years later, he had come up with a means to keep his rocket from drifting all over the desert sky. Continuing to annually reread Wells's *The War of the Worlds* he kept dreaming, kept hoping.

Funding for Goddard's Roswell experiments came principally from financier Harry Guggenheim, who had been advised of Goddard's work by famed aviator Charles Lindbergh. By 1932, however, the Great Depression had severely eroded Guggenheim's money supply. Disappointed but not broken, Goddard left New Mexico that year and went back to Clark University to teach. By 1934, with Guggenheim's finances solid once again, Goddard returned to Roswell. That same year, Lindbergh, who was serving as Guggenheim's technical adviser, and his wife, Anne, flew into Roswell to offer encouragement. The following year, Lindbergh and Guggenheim came together to Roswell for an inspection of Eden Valley. Wishing to impress his guests, Goddard tried three launches in the space of a couple of days. Frustratingly, all three were duds. Still, the observers from back East were pleased with the attempts.

Progress continued: in 1938, Goddard launched a rocket 6,565 feet. Oddly, in the years before the war, the United States government expressed no real interest in rockets. Then, suddenly, the news broke that the Germans possessed a powerful V-2 rocket. Almost indentical to Goddard's, the German rocket would eventually be fired at England with devastating results. Though Guggenheim's funds had vanished by the beginning of the war, the Navy now wanted to develop liquid fuel rocket motors for the war effort that would enable heavily loaded bombers and seaplanes to take off quickly. Would Goddard help?

Yes, Goddard answered, without hesitation. Would he move to Annapolis? That question took some thought. The Goddards hated to leave Roswell, which had grown on them. They loved the serenity, even the harshness of the land. Nonetheless, Robert wanted to remain productive and liked to be needed. So, in 1942 he left Eden Valley for the final time.

Goddard's Roswell residency lasted from 1930 to 1942. He performed fifty-six flight tests there, and each launch brought refinements and new designs. Through his work in Roswell, Goddard developed a varible-thrust rocket motor that could be controlled by a pilot. And in 1947, this motor became the basis for the X-1 rocket plane. Three months after the Roswell incident, Chuck Yeager, a slow-drawling, seemingly fearless West Virginia farmboy flew the X-1 fast enough to break the sound barrier, a feat long believed impossible.

Relocated in Maryland, Goddard missed the wide open spaces of Chaves County, New Mexico. So fond of Roswell were he and Esther that the couple discussed retiring there after the war. But Robert Goddard never made it back to New Mexico. He developed throat cancer, an affliction that had killed his father years before. Goddard underwent a laryngectomy, which robbed him of his voice but didn't cure him. He died at Johns Hopkins Hospital in Baltimore on August 10, 1945. He was sixty-two and was buried at Worcester, Massachusetts. The day before he died, Goddard had been strong enough to sit up in bed and read that a second nuclear bomb had been dropped, on Nagasaki. The bomb, he knew, had been tested at what later became known as Trinity Site, approximately 100 miles west of Roswell.

Goddard's contributions are many. He invented the mechanisms that propelled, stabilized, and guided the modern rocket. He endured setbacks and at the same time raised the rocket from a dangerous toy and sent it on its way to be an interplanetary vehicle. Goddard received eighty-three patents on his rocket and space ideas during his lifetime, and after his death his research notes resulted in 131 more patents. He laid the technical foundations for today's long-range rockets, missiles, earth satellites, and space flight, and came up with the basic designs for such launch vehicles as the Atlas, Thor, Jupiter, and Redstone rockets.

During the postwar years, Goddard's significance was not immediately recognized. But by the late 1950s, as the United States began to embark on space ventures, things changed, starting in Roswell. A wing that includes a planetarium at the Roswell Museum and Art Center was dedicated in Goddard's name in April

1959. Among items on display there is an 18-foot-long rocket that flew to an altitude of 3,294 feet over Roswell and then dropped slowly back to the sagebrush floor by parachute. The museum owns Goddard's original tools, too—his grinders, screwdrivers, drill presses, clamps, and crowbars. On a post in the Goddard wing hangs a calendar stuck at August 1931. Resurrected and standing in front of the museum is Goddard's 100-foot launch tower, from which he sent liquid propellent rockets to explore extreme altitudes. Some smaller items reside on public display at the Smithsonian Institution's National Air and Space Museum in Washington, D.C. Goddard's old house on Mescalero Road has become a private residence.

In 1970, when Roswell opened its second high school—the one Nancy Lopez would later be graduated from—the building bore Goddard's name and a mascot that surely would make the inventor proud: the Rockets.

Goddard finally received his due on the national level when, in 1961, the Goddard Space Flight Center, the National Aeronautics and Space Administration's electronic braincenter for all explorations, was opened in Greenbelt, Maryland.

Near the end of his life, Goddard no longer had looked toward Mars, but instead toward the moon. That goal first showed palpable influence after his death with the creation of one of the first science-fiction movies, *Destination Moon*, a precipitator of the fifties' cycle of sci-fi films. Released in 1950, *Destination Moon* was taken from the Robert A. Heinlein novel *Rocketship Galileo*, published in 1947. In that story, a scientist and three high school boys build an atomic rocket and make what they think is the first journey to the moon. Unbeknownst to them, Nazis have already arrived on the lunar surface. A decent movie even if it did point car headlights against black velvet backdrop to show the stars, *Destination Moon* focused on the race to use the moon as a rocket launch site. With typical Cold War naiveté, a general in *Destination Moon* announces, "The country that can launch missiles from the moon can control the Earth. That, gentlemen, is the most important military fact of this century."

It may appear odd, but *Destination Moon* owes more to Robert Goddard than to Robert Heinlein. *Destination Moon* has its real roots in 1929's *Die Frau in Mond* ("The Woman in the Moon"), the first authentic space travel movie, directed by Germany's Fritz Lang. As a technical advisor, Lang had used Hermann Oberth, the rocket scientist who corresponded with Goddard throughout the 1920s and who, many historians feel, stole most of the American's ideas.

Made for under $600,000 and fired across the screens on the fumes of Roswell, *Destination Moon* enjoyed great box-office success. Not surprisingly, it prompted the production of quickie imitations, such as *Rocketship X-M* (1950) and *Flight to Mars* (1951). Al Capp's *L'il Abner* comic strip even hopped up on the launch pad, in 1950. With corncob pipe firmly stuck between her teeth, Mammy Yokum straddles a Goddard-looking rocket and roars off to Planet Pincus No. 7, an orb inhabited by mechanical men.

Goddard's dream of touching down on Mars, Venus, or the moon, which he thought could be done for only one million dollars, remained out of reach until 1961. President John F. Kennedy that year recognized the nation should "commit itself to achieving the goal before this decade is out of landing a man on the moon and returning him safely to Earth . . . this is a new ocean and I believe the United States must sail upon it." As astronaut missions followed that directive through the 1960s, space travel, as envisioned by Roswell-inspired Robert Goddard, became further entwined with popular culture. When The Byrds sang "Mr. Spaceman" in 1966, the group made it plain that extraterrestrial life was entirely possible:

> Woke up this morning with that light in my eyes,
> and then realized it was still dark outside.
> It was a light comin' down from the sky.
> I don't know who or why.

Must be those strangers that come every night,
whose saucer shaped light put people uptight.
Leave blue green footprints that glow in the dark,
I hope they get home all right.

Nearly everyone, it seemed, wanted to be part of the great adventure, and space travel soon stood as a metaphor for this country's pioneering spirit. Though Robert Goddard enjoyed joining
Esther at the picture show in Roswell, it is anyone's guess what
he would have thought of such space travel adventures as *The
Mouse on the Moon* (1963), about a tiny country that discovers its
homemade wine makes excellent rocket fuel; or *Santa Claus Con-
quers the Aliens* (1964), in which actress Pia Zadora helps to prove
that one jolly old white-haired man is tougher than a lot of little
gray men. Nor can one imagine what Goddard would have said
upon learning that a New Mexico-trained chimpanzee took a 15-
minute space flight in 1961, that an astronaut played golf on the
moon in 1969, or that *Star Trek* creator Gene Roddenberry, before he died in 1991, asked that his ashes be fired into deep space.
Roddenberry's request, which was granted by NASA, by the way,
surely would generate lively conversation at Roswell lunch counters,
where it's likely that almost everything oddball has at some point
been discussed.

"Say, any idea what the cost is of having your remains blasted
to kingdom come?"

"Beats me. Where does a fella go to get that done, anyhow?"

When it arrived in bookstores in 1969, Norman Mailer's *Of a
Fire on the Moon* told people about rockets and their power in ways
Goddard could not have imagined as he tracked his first launches
skyward in the 1930s. Same with Tom Wolfe's *The Right Stuff*, which
came along a decade after *Of a Fire on the Moon*. Both books used
language in new ways to justify and demystify the space movement not only to Roswellians, but to millions of Americans. *Of a
Fire on the Moon* showed Mailer's dazzling skills, but the nonfiction

work revealed the Author as Alter-Astronaut. Mailer, writing in the third person, under the name Aquarius, managed to make himself as important in this treatment as the men who actually go to the moon. It's a technique that surely could only have evolved through the free-spirited structure of New Journalism, a voice and form that originated and was refined during this period of popular culture.

> The ship of space was after all not one rocket, but essentially two—a brain on the end of a firecracker is how Aquarius first vulgarly would seize the idea of it—but actually it was composed of two rockets, one on top of the other, separate rockets each possessed of brain and force of propulsion. It was just that the lower rocket, the first rocket, the mighty rocket which would lift it into the air, while not entirely without a brain, had in effect the little skull which sits on the neck of a dinosaur, and the second rocket, which would travel to the moon, while almost unimaginably intelligent (and pregnant as well with a mechanical child who would reach a new land) was also possessed of its own sources of fire. In comparison to the dinosaur called Saturn, the power which propelled Apollo's brain was modest, it was in fact about one four-hundredth of the initial force which would lift the two rockets Apollo and Saturn together but this small motor was still powerful enough to propel Apollo through all of its intricately conceived plans and projects.

Another legacy from Goddard's stay in Roswell offers a sad counterpoint to the virtuoso images Mailer employed. Within a forty-mile radius of the city stand twelve empty Atlas Intercontinental missile silos, the grim discards of America's Cold War. The seventy-five-foot long Atlas F missile, once the pride of the

United States government, was obsolete before it was deployed. It later was replaced by such missiles as the Pershing, the Minuteman III and the Polaris. But at the time of its installation in the 1960s, the Atlas F was the world's most powerful—and expensive—surface-to-surface intercontinental ballistic missile. Its silo alone cost $34 million.

From the beginning in 1960 trouble plagued the Atlas F project. The silos, about 180 feet deep, suffered water-pump problems and never really worked properly. On February 16, 1961, a 20-ton crane used by workers to lower steel into holes in the ground, plunged into a silo about twenty-six miles northeast of Roswell and burst into flames. Six men died in the accident and fourteen others were injured.

The Atlas F sites, chosen for their remoteness and proximity to Roswell's atomic-sensitive Walker Air Force Base, operated for about four years. Eventually, the Air Force began to phase out the missiles and all the silos were abandoned, in 1965, the year they were completed. Curiously, the Atlas F used liquid oxygen, as its main propellant fuel, the same fuel that Goddard had promoted long before. However, the dangers and volatility of liquid oxygen led technicians to use a solid fuel propellant on the Atlas F successor, the Minuteman series.

Rocketry in southeast New Mexico didn't suffer when Goddard left. Indeed, his mantle was picked up at the end of World War II by another rocket scientist, Wernher von Braun. The two men could not have been more unlike. Mousy and reticent, Goddard was not fond of the public eye. Handsome and extroverted, von Braun reveled in the spotlight and loved talking to the public. Here is Mailer on the scientist:

> . . . shaking hands, he had obvious funds of charisma. "You must help us give a shove to the program," he said to Aquarius on greeting. . . . Yes, von Braun most definitely was not like other men. Curiously shifty, as

if to show his eyes in full would give away much too much, he offered the impression of a man who wheeled whole complexes of caution into every gesture—he was after all an engineer who put massive explosives into adjoining tanks and then was obliged to worry about leaks.

While living in Nazi Germany before and during the war, where he worked with Hermann Oberth, von Braun helped to develop the V-2 rocket. But von Braun's association with Oberth, "the father of space travel," goes back even farther, to the late 1920s. Von Braun, Oberth and Willy Ley, who would also gain glory as a spokesman for space conquest, originally were part of a team that put cats inside suitcases and then fired the bags down rocket sled tracks on the outskirts of Berlin. Many historians believe Oberth and his prodigy von Braun later lifted Goddard's principles. In fact, Goddard complained that much of his mail from and to Roswell during the thirties appeared to have been tampered with and some letters might have even disappeared. Though Goddard, a true follower of H.G. Wells, obviously believed in life on other planets, he never publicly spoke about it. However, Oberth did. In 1954, the German scientist said UFOs were "conceived and directed by intelligent beings of a very high order, and they are propelled by distorting the gravitational field, converting gravity to usable energy."

If Obeth admired Goddard, von Braun clearly worshipped him. On July 13, 1960, a granite marker was dedicated at Goddard's Aunt Effie's strawberry farm in Auburn, Massachusetts, now a golf course. The marker noted the spot as being the launch site for the world's first liquid propellant rocket flight. In the audience that summer afternoon was Wernher von Braun, a celebrity by now who had defected from Germany. In fact, von Braun served as a speaker that day, and referred to Goddard as his "boyhood hero."

Von Braun's arrival in the United States will always be viewed as controversial. After the war ended, von Braun and a team of German rocket scientists were allowed to enter the United States to continue their work on the V-2 at White Sands Proving Grounds, southwest of Roswell. There the men assembled and checked out V-2s brought over from Germany, and at the same time trained American soldiers in the art and science of rocketry. Additionally, the Germans advised representatives of industrial firms interested in becoming active in the rocket and missile field. During von Braun's five years at White Sands, dozens of V-2s carrying instruments designed to study the upper atmosphere, solar radiation, and the frontiers of space were successfully launched in New Mexico. It's uncertain whether von Braun actually visited Roswell, though it's possible he did because Walker Air Force Base at the time headquartered the management of atomic groups. Photographs, however, do exist of von Braun and his German rocket team relaxing on a holiday—by wearing three-piece suits!—while at nearby Lincoln, New Mexico, a town made famous by Billy the Kid.

Though it's a known fact that von Braun was working in White Sands when the Roswell incident occurred, many UFO students completely disregard the coincidence. Indeed, if you queried most people in Roswell about von Braun, they might remember him from his days as a television guest on *The Walt Disney Show,* where he regularly chatted with the host and filled Disney in about advancements in space travel. Through Disney, a generation of young Americans who listened to von Braun likely believed that space flight had a Teutonic accent. Still, there is no denying that if von Braun launched a V-2 rocket from White Sands and it veered off course by, say, 30 degrees, it could easily have landed north of Roswell and made the explosion heard in July 1947.

Wernher von Braun died in 1977 at age sixty-five. Considered a scientific giant in most people's eyes—his three-stage Saturn rocket helped to take America to the moon—some never forgot that he was at one time an active member of the Nazi party and a major in the SS during the war. If his past haunted him, von Braun never let it be known. He had a job to do, and he did it—spreading the gospel of space flight that had been started in Roswell by Robert Hutchings Goddard.

And today, spreading the word about Roswell is big business.

chapter 3

Let Us Gather at the (Pecos) River

"Roswell is booming!"
—*Leeza*, 1997

 ROSWELL, TUESDAY, JULY 1:

8 A.M.: "UFO SUCKERS—69 CENTS," says a candy store advertisement in the special UFO Encounter '97 supplement published
by the *Roswell Daily Record*. Perhaps it is fitting that the newspaper that in 1947 helped to start the flying saucer fuss should sum
things up fifty years later.

There's no business like UFO business. The bandwagon, car-
nival commercialism of Encounter '97 is visible this first day up
and down Roswell's Main Street. Church's Fried Chicken has a
"Best Alien Chicken in Town" sign; Tastee Freez: "Our Food is
Out of This World;" Big O Tires: "E.T. Phone Home." Dining es-
tablishments boast UFO margaritas, UFO burritos, UFO cookies.
"NO VACANCY" signs deck the horizon and rickety card tables
residents have set up and decorated with homemade placards that
resemble a kid's lemonade kiosk jumble the sidewalks. "Alien rocks,"
cries a crude banner a Roswellian has attached to a pile of gravel
likely scraped from his driveway. "Alien slime" and "Alien goo"

indicate hand-scrawled labels on used miniature liquor bottles filled with a strange-looking sediment. By week's end, all will be sold. So will every jar of hand-spooned "Mighty Martian Mustard (with a solar taste)."

Over in the media room at the Convention and Civic Center officials are handing out credentials like M&M's: Vulcan Network? Sure, here's two press passes. Turkish TV? Glad to have you with us. Radio Buenos Aires? Find your room OK? The media—more than 300 will show up, but so far about 100 members—are quickly herded into buses and are among the first group taken to the alleged crash site which, it turns out, is one of at least four suspected crash sites. But this is the one Roswell supports. Located about thirty miles from town, the site is a vast hard sprawl, a home for sheep, cattle, and rattlesnakes.

The Corn family, owners of the land, has lived in the area since 1879. Way, way back, Martin Van Buren Corn raised horses and one of those animals was sold to noted lawman Pat Garrett. Billy the Kid, New Mexico's best known historical figure, then stole the horse from Garrett during The Kid's murderous breakout from the Lincoln County Jail in 1880. The Corns purchased this particular parcel—twenty-four square miles—in 1976. About six years ago, the Corns kept noticing strangers driving about, not in grime-caked pickups with gunracks, but in gleaming Chryslers with out-of-state plates. When Miller "Hub" Corn asked what they wanted, he learned that his land likely lay where a flying saucer crash-landed in July 1947. Since then, the Corns, who will tell you that ranching is not an easy way to make a living, will also tell you that they have bear-hugged UFOs. The family charges fifteen dollars per person to enter. "I could be a real hard-butt and lock the gate," says Hub, "but people will still get in."

As he watches the first media bus unload this bright, lifeless morning, Hub Corn, thirty-six, stands by quietly, a sunburned, soft-talking fellow in a gimme cap. Alongside him rise two huge stone obelisks, which he had erected a few weeks before. The obelisks mark the beginning of a trail that leads to the site.

"Normally," says Hub, "at this time of year we are hauling hay or planting sorghum. I've got somebody else taking care of that for me, while I do this." Down a path from the obelisks sits a boulder, the base of which is decorated with bouquets of flowers. Carved into the rock are these lines:

> We Don't Know Who They Were
> We Don't Know Why They Came
> We Only Know
> They Changed Our View
> Of the Universe
> This Universal Sacred Site
> Is Dedicated July 1997
> To the Beings
> Who Met Their Destiny
> Near Roswell, N.M. July 1947

"At first I thought it was all a bunch of bull," says Hub. "But then I got to studyin' and researchin' and I found out it was true." So convinced was Hub that he went out and got for the family Suburban a vanity license plate that reads "BELIEVE." According to many reports, the craft first impacted twenty-five miles west of where the Corns live. The spaceship, some researchers say, got struck by lightning. Others believe it got messed up by our radar system. The consensus is that it tobogganed across what is known as the debris field and kept going until it smacked into the side of a ridge that faces the big rock now carved in tribute. "It was a triangular shaped thing, something like the heel of a shoe," says Hub Corn. "Twenty-two by twenty feet."

While cameras click and camcorders whir, Hub goes on: "There were three bodies on the inside that were half in and half out.

Supposedly one alien was alone sitting on that rock yonder. Some people say they kept him alive. They say he was holding a little black box when the military showed up and they had to bang him on the head with a rifle butt to get that box away from him."

When the military arrived, troops moving shoulder to shoulder quickly combed the area clean, the story goes. Although many UFO champions consider Roswell to be the best-documented case of an extraterrestrial encounter, not one authentic scrap of physical evidence remains at the site or, as far as can anyone can tell, in the hands of witnesses. A widely held theory has the military picking up every piece of lint two days before ranch foreman Mack Brazel came into town with the debris he had recovered. When Brazel showed up, the whole story just exploded, according to disciples. "That old guy," muses Hub Corn, "he opened up the can of worms."

A reporter asks Corn how many people have paid the fifteen dollars to visit the site. "I don't like to quote numbers," says Corn, "because I get hammered by the IRS." Another writer wonders why the Jim McKnights, the longtime owners of the land who sold the property to the Corns, never talked of a saucer coming here. The McKnights even said later that there were no roads in here in 1947 so it would have been extremely difficult for a military clean-up crew to enter.

Hub Corn strokes his moustache and shrugs. He doesn't know about those details—"There's so many names in this incident I forget 'em all." Instead, he has his own story, which buoys him during baffling times. "I seen some things out here that are questionable. I bale a lot of alfalfa hay. We do it at night. I was out near here at 2:30 one morning about five or six years ago. I busted a shear bolt in the baler and got off and started walking to the tractor. A couple of hundred yards away this thing, with eight or nine bright lights on it, was twenty to thirty feet off the ground. Out here, there aren't any lights. So here's this thing, it wasn't making any sound, basically sitting there, just hovering. I just crossed my arms and waited and it took off and I thought it was going to hit my house. The next morning I asked my wife if she heard anything and she said no. I asked our hired man and he said no. I proceeded to tell that story and they thought I was full of it."

Corn's tale over, the press begins to wander off. Joachim Beck, who works for a television network in Munich, Germany, stares at the carved rock and says, "The interesting thing to me is that they've turned this into a festival. They're so honest about it. The mayor, he says, 'Why shouldn't we make money?'" Sitting on the ground nearby, a producer from Fort Lauderdale, Florida, suddenly howls in pain. It's a voice that sounds distinctly like a man who has just watched an alien erupt from his sternum. "What the hell are these?" he yells as he plucks from his socks tiny spiked burrs. "Space balls?" No one answers the man because few have heard of *Tribulus terrestris*, the state weed of New Mexico. Unofficially, the troublesome things are known as "goatheads."

At that point, the Corns' big Suburban takes off across the desert, with Hub's wife, Sheila, at the wheel. Earlier, Sheila had helped Hub take tickets and answer questions. "Where's she going?" a reporter wonders. "To the bank," comes a reply.

3 P.M.: Inside the International UFO Museum and Research Center, which has taken over the old Plains Theater in Roswell, Terry Warnecke, an astrologist from Phoenix, is giving a talk to an audience of about 150. If Warnecke wants to be taken seriously, he has stationed himself in a peculiar spot in the museum. Looking directly down on him are cardboard cutouts of R2D2 and Chewbacca, figures from the movie *Star Wars*. Twenty feet away the museum's Alien Caffeine Espresso Bar does a brisk business.

Warnecke, who was born in 1947, says a new radio beacon in the Four Corners area caused at least four UFO crashes that year, including two saucers that struck one another. "Somehow, they inadvertently collided. Roswell is the end product of a big air disaster. They (aliens) couldn't call home or make it back home. Thank

God they didn't take it out on us. The pilots of those spacecraft were in trouble. Some very possibly lived and were taken captive. Fifty years have gone by, so they're probably not with us."

By calling attention to its "research" facilities, the International UFO Museum attempts to lure the legitimate investigator. And yet the museum gift shop sells UFO playing cards for $6.95 and posts on the wall such cartoons as "The Mother Ship Has Landed" that shows white-haired women deplaning and giving these orders to their sons: "Dress warm!" "Try My Meat Loaf" "What's Wrong With a Second Helping?" and "How Come You Never Call?"

Across the room, barrel-chested Walter Haut, the ex-Army Air Corps officer who wrote the famous "Flying Disk Recovered" press release in 1947, begins one of the 250 or so interviews he will give this week. He already looks weary. Glenn Dennis, the snowy-haired former mortician who says the military asked him in 1947 about the availability of child-sized caskets, walks by in an appropriately funereal black suit, signing autographs as he goes. At the other end of the building, Stanton Friedman, the bushy-browed author of three books on the Roswell incident, is either reminding awestruck groupies around him that he is a trained nuclear physicist and thus has an intimacy with UFOs, or he is reciting to anyone who will listen this mantra: "A lot of people in Roswell were told, 'If you talk, we'll kill you and your whole family.'"

8 P.M.: Kevin Randle strides to the lectern in the Roswell Inn's main ballroom. A former Air Force officer who has also written three books about Roswell, Randle, with a graying moustache and a glint in his eye, looks like a riverboat gambler. "We may have reached the point of diminishing returns in terms of witnesses," he announces. Randle has spent years trying to find people who knew people who might know people who could have been in Roswell. Reportedly, there was an archaeologist near the crash site, says Randle, a Dr. Holden, and when Randle finally found the man, Holden was ninety-six and barely remembered his own name.

Randle couldn't find Barney Barnett, another alleged witness to another Roswell crash, because Barnett had died of throat cancer, a fact Randle positively attributes to searing radiation that apparently comes from a flying saucer.

10 P.M.: Bud's Bar, a tavern on the north end of Roswell, promotes itself as the "Unofficial UFO Crash Recovery Site." Inside, Bud's provides a cozy place to cool off and hear the latest UFO yuk. "Know what's a close encounter of the fifth kind?" asks a well-digger in a flannel shirt with the sleeves slashed off. When no one can tell him, the well-digger points to a shelf behind the bar on which sits a large bottle of Jack Daniel's.

WEDNESDAY, JULY 2

10 A.M.: On the edge of what used to be Walker Air Force Base, inside what used to be a video shop, stands the modest, funky UFO Enigma Museum. John Price, the owner, is a bearded, lanky, former roofer who says his museum was the first in town. Price, in fact, doesn't like some of the gents who started the other, bigger museum. Indeed, he's been at war with them and with the Chamber of Commerce which, he says, for a time cut him out of their promotions and wouldn't even mention his museum to Roswell visitors. Price has gotten revenge. He's written his own book, *Roswell: A Quest for the Truth*.

Territorialism runs through the Roswell UFO research field. Members of this specialization often go from one symposium to another, disagreeing on crash site locales, guarding the latest third-hand witness, stirring up more theories, envying colleagues. Kevin Randle and Don Schmitt co-authors of Roswell books, barely speak. Schmitt, a postman from Wisconsin, has been accused in print by another researcher, Phil Klass, of falsifying college credentials, and the revelation caused Randle great embarrassment. In turn, Randle doesn't much care for Max Littell, an International UFO

Museum official who pushes another crash site because, some say, Hub Corn wouldn't sell *his* site to the museum. William Moore, co-author of *The Roswell Incident*, has all sorts of critics because many believe he embellished the MJ-12, a presidential-appointed body supposedly ordered to look into Roswell in 1947, though Moore denies the hoax. Few Roswell researchers think much of Philip Corso, the former Army officer who has just written *The Day After Roswell*, a book that is selling well despite the fact that Corso says he once met aliens in a cave. International UFO Museum founder Glenn Dennis has been accused of changing his story several times over the years, and Walter Haut, faultfinders point out, is simply interested in making change from his story. (That Haut drives a fancy, new BMW with a "MR UFO" license plate may have something to do with catty remarks hurled his way.)

It's hard, however, to dislike John Price. Though not well-educated, Price is clever. His museum this day is selling "Area 51" badges. For ten dollars you can get your photograph taken and then have it fitted into a badge that says "Top Security Clearance" at the Area 51 site, which many visitors are surprised to find out, lies not in Roswell, but in Nevada where, allegedly, the government kept saucers, a notion the government has called absurd.

1 P.M. In the media room, a photojournalist from Sweden asks Encounter '97 director Stan Crosby what else is there to do in Roswell after you've seen the crash site. Crosby, a wavy-haired former oil and gas developer testily suggests visiting the International UFO Museum and Research Center, which his wife, Deon, just happens to direct. Waving a program of the week's events, a broadcaster from Canada wonders what a cow-milking contest has do with Roswell. "There are a hundred dairies in the area," Crosby snaps. A reporter from Colorado asks Crosby if Roswell is the first UFO bash to be held in the U.S. Crosby isn't sure, but the answer is no. From 1953 to 1977, George Van Tassel, a former test pilot

for Lockheed and author of *I Rode a Flying Saucer*, put on the Giant Rock Spacecraft Convention near Palm Springs, California. During its day, the event mirrored Roswell. The *Los Angeles Times* reported 10,000 people attended some years in the mid-fifties. An accompanying *Times* photograph showed a sea of attendees wearing floppy hats, sitting in lawn chairs, and listening to guest speakers. On sale were autographed books and such Roswell-like kitsch as UFO ashtrays and packets of hair from a Venusian dog. Van Tassel purportedly received his orders to hold the convention from a spaceman named Solganda. One year, according to the *Times*, Prince Neasom and his wife Princess Negonna, from the planet of Tythan, eight and a half light years away, made a special appearance. Roswell has yet to have the pleasure of such royalty.

3 P.M.: Lance Strong Eagle Crawford, a member of the Southern Ute tribe, delivers the Indian perspective: "My grandfather told me that everyone, including the Light People, is one in the universe." That notion advanced, this news follows: Dancers from Laguna Pueblo will hold a special ceremony at Hub Corn's ranch—to consecrate the crash site. Meanwhile, newspapers are reporting this morning that up in the northwest corner of New Mexico, Navajos are railing about white men who want their ashes buried on the moon—a holy orb to that tribe.

4 P.M.: A Korean TV journalist is interviewing Greta McDonald, an aide in the media room whose chief job is replenishing a box of pastries. "There's a great number of foreign press here," explains McDonald, "because overseas they have so much more understanding of these things. In the States, everybody is from Missouri."

6 P.M.: Deon Crosby to a CNN newsman: "We've been spoofing this for a couple of years now, but from now on we're gonna force feed it on the people whether they like it or not."

10 P.M.: Roswell has a history as a home for hustlers. After all, Van Smith, founder of the city, was a professional gambler. At Bud's Bar this night, Jimmy, an ex-schoolteacher in Roswell, reveals his scam to an interested audience. Earlier this day Jimmy says he took a ten dollar bill and pasted an alien's face over Alexander Hamilton's. Then he went to Kinko's and ran off 100 copies. Though the souvenir bills are badly faded and look less realistic than Monopoly money, this afternoon Jimmy says he sold fifty of them— at a dollar each.

THURSDAY, JULY 3

9 A.M.: KGFL—1400 on the AM dial—was the Roswell radio station that first received Walter Haut's celebrated press release that told of the capture of a flying saucer in 1947. The station is long gone. In its place now is KCRX, a "memories" station. Not oldies from the fifties or sixties, but tunes from, well, 1947, such as Tex Williams's "Smoke, Smoke, Smoke That Cigarette." That song might well serve as the theme for saucer lovers, many of whom puff non-stop as if the burden to believe is too stressful. They have role models, these believers. Jesse Marcel Sr., the RAAF security officer in the center of the 1947 storm, never was photographed without a cigarette in his hand. In the same manner, The Cigarette-Smoking Man is a chief supporting character on the *The X-Files.*

10 A.M.: Erich von Daniken, author of the 1969 blockbuster *Chariots of the Gods?* has published twenty-two books, but wonders, "I am not a UFO man. So what, for goodness sakes, am I doing here? With Roswell, all we have is controversy. I don't know what is true. If it took place, I could relate it to the returning of the gods."

God bless Roswell. With more than 100 houses of worship in town, Roswell is a church-going city. Some churches are happy to have the visitors: St. Mark's Evangelism Lutheran offers free coffee to anyone driving down Main Street. Some churches are more wary: The Church of Christ marquee says, "Aliens? Maybe— God? Definitely." To fundamentalist Christians, the idea of demon-inspired beings threatens the creationist viewpoint. To the less dogmatic, Roswell can be explained by the Bible: the prophet Ezekiel, after all, speaks of four humanlike creatures, accompanied by wheels that moved with them. There's nothing, of course, in the Bible to explain *Invasion of the Space Preachers*, a 1990 film that has human-like aliens taking money from righteous hillbillies. Conversely, the movie version of *The War of the Worlds* (1953) is one of the most religious of all UFO films. Fleeing angry Martians, mobs of people in the movie take refuge in a church. When the Martians, who have arrived on Earth in spaceships that look like a cross between a cobra and a gooseneck lamp, finally expire, voices ring out an Amen chorus.

Karl Travis, the thirty-something minister at Roswell's Westminster Presbyterian Church, has watched with puzzled concern what has gone on in town the last few days: "This conference is just an exercise in preaching to the choir." Travis says his attitude about UFOs is like his attitude about the Second Coming. "We're not supposed to spend a great deal of time waiting for it. I don't think Jesus is coming back on a flying saucer. This whole thing is not a faith issue. I'm a fan of *The X-Files*, and I think something happened. But I don't spend a lot of time dwelling on what."

Travis is more bothered by the arrogance that the incident inspires. "Our local TV anchors, who are new to town, smirk the entire time UFO news comes on. And the *Time* magazine cover story? The guy who wrote that came here with an agenda. He says when he stepped off the plane in Roswell he smelled a 'manure-like' substance. It *was* manure, you damn Yankee!"

A good portion of Roswell wants the UFO Encounter to go away and let Roswell go back to being a dishwater-dull community. Chagrin is also detectable in Roswell. Several members of Karl Travis's congregation have made sure they are out of town during Encounter '97. They were afraid of the traffic, the crowds, the lines, the fun-poking. "Kook City," *USA Today* called Roswell.

Q: Do you need a passport or visa to get into Roswell?

A: Just a Visa card.

In a way, Roswell's reputation has become like its tiny neighbor just down the highway, Lake Arthur, New Mexico. On October 5, 1977, Maria Rubio, a Lake Arthur housewife, was preparing a breakfast burrito at home for her husband Eduardo, a farmworker, when she suddenly gasped, then stopped. Tattooed to an edge of one tortilla was a singe mark that for all the world resembled the face of Jesus, topped by a crown of thorns. Maria Rubio made sure to save that piece of food and as word of its existence spread, people started flocking to the Rubios small home to see the face in the flour. Hundreds of people, then thousands. They lined up to get in the door and some even crawled through the windows. The story was broadcast around the world, and eventually Maria's children, though proud of their mother, were upset by what had transpired. Like Roswell and a UFO, Lake Arthur became synonymous with Jesus and a tortilla. In time, the Rubio children refused to tell new acquaintances exactly where they were from. "Southeastern New Mexico," they would answer vaguely.

If inhabitants of Roswell are uneasy about their town's notoriety, there is not much they can do. Full-page display advertisements have begun appearing in nationally circulated publications this week. One ad shows a jet-propelled vodka bottle sailing over a barren desert. The headline reads: "Absolut Roswell." Another ad features a couple in a station wagon, lost and suddenly confronted with a flying saucer. Nearby is a compass and a road map, open to Roswell. The headline: "Honey, Where's the Ericsson Cellular Phone?"

Could anyone really get lost on the way to Roswell? Yes. It's been reported that some visitors this week actually wound up in Roswell, Georgia, an Atlanta suburb. Inquiring about accommodations, one tourist even telephoned Buffalo, New York's Roswell Park Cancer Institute.

Roswell's Madison Avenue magnetism, in fact, can be found as far back as 1957. A Nestle's chocolate campaign that year featured Neddy Nestle, who was taken from his bed one night by little green men. The visitors gently pushed Neddy toward their spaceship— the "Jumpin' Jupiter Saucer Service"—until he finally got them to let go. How? He simply steered his abductors into the kitchen for a cup of Nestle's cocoa.

11 A.M.: "You know, I just may try to sell some T-shirts on the street," cracks Colin McMillan. Hawking gewgaws is for many residents an economic necessity in Roswell. After all, the town's median income is twenty-seven percent below the national average. The jobless rate is more than seven percent. However, to see Colin McMillan pushing keepsake tank tops would be a strange sight, for he doesn't need the extra income, nice as it might be. For ten years, McMillan was a state representative out of Roswell and he ran unsuccessfully in 1994 for the U.S. Senate. For two years he served as assistant secretary of defense under President George Bush. A geophysicist who owns his own oil exploration business around the corner from the International UFO Museum and Research Center, McMillan is a voice of reason during Encounter '97. He has no plans to attend any of the events or to cut into the merchandising. "I've got more pressing business," he explains. On this morning, even though it is already close to 100 degrees, he is heading off to play golf.

The temperature, in fact, has been more than 100 all week. Hot enough, as Roswell old-timers might put it, to melt a snake. A local disc jockey each steamy day this week has been asking the same critical question: "Why couldn't that saucer have crashed in October?"

2 P.M.: Mary Matalin is hosting her nationally syndicated radio talk show from Main Street's Cattle Baron restaurant. On the air Matalin listens as New Mexico governor Gary Johnson tells her

that soon after he was elected to office he was taken to a secluded basement where some officials told him in furtive tones what happened in Roswell in 1947. Then Matalin tells Johnson that her husband, James Carville, a political consultant with reptilian facial features, didn't want to join her in New Mexico and now she knows why. "All James's relatives are in Roswell."

Matalin's principal guest is Walter Haut, closing in on his sixtieth interview. Matalin calls him Walter "Hot" and is not corrected, even though the name is pronounced "Hought." Indeed, Haut will also hear "Hoot" "Hoat" and "Hute" this week. He'll be asked what kind of typewriter he used to bang out that memorable press release and even what he had for lunch that July day a half century ago.

7 P.M.: A special presentation of the movie *Roswell* is taking place at the Del Norte Twin Theaters. In a way, the movie first brought this circus to town, in 1995. When *Roswell* appeared on cable TV in 1994, Roswell city administrators were flustered to learn that the movie had been filmed in Arizona. From then on, Roswell officials vowed to try to line city pockets with anything connected to the incident, and to align the city with all things alien. For instance, the mayor's official stationary now contains a flying-saucer shaped watermark. *Roswell*, which proudly bills itself the recipient of a Golden Globe nomination as best TV film of 1994, highlights the alleged cover-up and so perhaps, appropriately, more toupees turn up on screen than can be seen in a Men's Hair Club infomercial. Coincidentally, a delightful and more logical movie, also titled *Roswell*, is being shown at the same time, inside the creaky annex of the Roswell Museum and Art Center. No rugs here. This version of *Roswell* is a twenty-minute animation made by a young, laid-back Harvard graduate from Texas named Bill Brown. In Brown's creation, the Roswell incident is blamed on a teenaged alien who borrowed his father's flying saucer without permission and took it for a joyride.

10 P.M.: An orange-haired, fortyish woman wearing a "I Came To Roswell and All I Got Was This Lousy Shirt" announces in Bud's Bar that she started to believe in UFOs the day President Jimmy Carter admitted he had seen one. But didn't Carter also claim, responds a listener, that a giant swimming rabbit once jumped into a boat and attacked him?

FRIDAY, JULY 4

9 A.M.: Paunchy and rumpled, Paul Davids is executive producer and co-writer of the Hollywood movie *Roswell*. The film apparently changed Davids into the character Richard Dreyfuss played in *Close Encounters of the Third Kind*. UFOs are now, it seems, all Davids thinks and talks about. "How's this?" asks Davids, as he unloads a bombshell. To a jammed auditorium at the New Mexico Military Institute, Davids announces that he has a fragment from the wreckage of the Roswell crash. He says he has had the piece tested, that it passed every scientific examination, and that he's now going to send the results to President Clinton. The words are enough to make the audience screech. Not so fast, please: when someone a year before said he came upon a purported Roswell UFO fragment, the news created similar Richter-scale shock waves. That fragment, kept in the Roswell Police Department's safe for a while, occasionally went on view at the International UFO Museum and Research Center. Eventually, it was learned that the piece had been fashioned in a Utah jeweler's workshop. Moreover, when the publisher of *Penthouse* magazine said he had photos of an alien autopsy done in Roswell in 1947, the images turned out to be props from the movie *Roswell*.

Davids won't reveal how or why he came upon his fragment or even if he has it with him. He does, however, show to the audience a slide of the object, which looks for all the world remarkably like a charcoal briquet.

10 A.M.: The UFO Expo—Encounter '97's marketplace—has opened inside the Roswell Convention and Civic Center. Twenty-four vendors had set up booths at the 1996 event here. This year, almost 130 merchants are on hand. Most of the items for sale have the word *alien* on them and most come with an alien's face, that familiar pointy skull bearing elliptical black eyes.

There are: alien backscratchers, alien balloons, alien beef jerky, alien Bibles, alien birdfeeders, alien body glitter, alien bookends, alien bookmarks, alien boxer shorts, alien burritos, alien Christmas stockings, alien coasters, alien clocks, alien doormats, alien ear cleaners, alien eggs, alien fetuses, alien finger puppets, alien gourds, alien green cards, alien jean jackets, alien kites, alien light switches, alien litter bags, alien lollipops, alien lottery tickets, alien mail pouches, alien nightlites, aliens on a cross, aliens on a toilet, alien pajamas, alien pennants, alien perfume, alien pewter earrings, alien piñatas, alien pinup mudflaps, alien placemats, alien pocket-knives, alien popcorn, alien potholders, alien pretzels, alien Santas, alien scarecrows, alien silly putty, alien snowdomes, alien shaved ice, alien tote bags, alien vases, alien voodoo dolls, alien windchimes, alien yard sculpture, alien yo-yos.

There are T-shirts with Elvis as an alien that say "I'm All Shook Up," and T-shirts with an alien on a Harley Davidson, and T-shirts with an alien contemplating the head of Albert Einstein. There is UFO wine, UFO squeeze bottles, UFO H2O. There are model kits of the saucer that crashed in Roswell for fifteen dollars, and a life-sized saucer on sale for $3,000. There are Alien Autopsy Games—for two to four players, ages eight to adult, batteries not included; and a UFO coloring book that has an alien on the cover ramming a thermometer up a human's nose. There is artwork of Grant Wood's "American Gothic," featuring aliens, and UFO Abduction Insurance ("Don't Leave Home Without It") offering a $100,000,000 policy. "The Truth Is Out There" bumper stickers are moving fast, though the truth, as most everybody knows, is right here—at the never-idle cash registers.

"We've taken advantage of the UFO phenomenon in a tasteful way," Roswell Chamber of Commerce president George Ruth tells a reporter from Detroit. As Ruth says this, crowds flood out of the Convention Center and charge toward a patio where more vendors have set up shop. The U.S. Postal Service is pushing envelopes prestamped from Roswell. There are Rozzie dolls on sale under an awning, though it's difficult to imagine Rozzie having the staying power of Barbie, which has been around since 1959 and has sold more than one billion. "The Roswell Incident," sung by Suzanne McDermott, a Judy Collins-soundalike, has just been released (I know what I saw and I know that we are not alone . . .) UFOs have long attracted musicians. In the 1970s, Elton John recorded the single "I've Seen the Saucers," not to be confused with Jefferson Airplane's "Have You Seen the Saucers?" The initial flying saucer ballad, however, was "The Disc Song," by Lucille Aghasian. Riding the crest of Roswell, it hit the airwaves in 1950:

> Pull the lever, look out below, fasten your belt and away we go,
> the flying disc is a modern machine, the way it works is
> a scientist's dream, it flies you to planets, to have a time,
> and if your Mom insists, you can be back by nine.

NOON: Dr. John Mack, a Harvard psychiatrist with a row of pens in his shirt pocket and an earnest but haggard expression on his long face, says three percent of Americans believe they have been abducted by aliens. Mack has been all over the world to interview abductees, including a Zulu tribesman who claims he made love to an outer space creature. ("She smelled bad"). That Mack has credentials from Harvard lends great credibility to the Roswell gathering. However, as someone points out, Timothy Leary was also a Harvard shrink. Far more convincing is this fact: many of Mack's abductees report witnessing ancient hieroglyphics, the same sort of markings supposedly seen on the debris fetched from Roswell in 1947.

Believing in UFOs doesn't necessarily mean believing in abductions. Roswell researchers such as Kevin Randle and Stanton Friedman champion the existence of flying saucers. Getting them to side with those who talk of being yanked from homes and taken for a lift in a cigar-shaped spaceship is another matter. But those transports do happen, argues Mack and others. Did you know, abduction proponents ask, that NASA has a regulation (14CFR1211) that allows the government to detain, examine, and decontaminate anyone who comes in contact with a UFO or its occupant? If the person does not agree to be detained, he or she can be fined up to $5,000 or sentenced to a year in jail.

Whitley Strieber and Budd Hopkins, both of whom have made large sums of folding money from the retelling of abduction stories, follow Mack's appearance. They deliver further proof that getting whisked away by visitors happens about as often as the sun shines. Finally, a spectator asks, "Where's the best place to be abducted?" Ready answers aren't forthcoming, though a lone voice calls out, "Where no one can see it happen."

Enlightened remarks on abductions come in a book titled *The Tainted Truth: The Manipulation of Fact in America*. It must be noted that the author, Cynthia Crossen, was not invited to speak in Roswell. Crossen says that a 1991 Roper study showed that one of fifty adult Americans may have been abducted by a UFO. The 6,000 people surveyed were asked if any of a number of experiences had happened to them. If they said yes enough times, that strongly supported alien abductions. On the list were things like having seen, as a child, a terrifying figure in your closet. Or having found puzzling scars on your body. Or hearing the word *trondant*, a made-up word that has a secret meaning only you know.

4 P.M.: The tiny crossroads of Midway, New Mexico, just south of Roswell, is pulling in people with the same power as Hub Corn's ranch, to the north. The word is out that down at Midway you

can see UFOs in broad daylight—for six dollars and fifty cents a look. In early 1994, Midway brothers Jose and Manuel Escamillo claim to have used home video cameras to tape the flights of UFOs during the daytime. A variety of flying saucers were reportedly captured on film, images that were shown on the TV series *Hard Copy* in September 1994. In one sequence, a dark shape resembling a helicopter transforms into a bright disk as it moves through the air. Some cynics have but two words for the Midway saucers: flying insects.

7 P.M.: Rain falls steadily as Whitley Strieber gives the keynote address of Encounter '97 at an aged hangar that was once part of Roswell Army Air Field. The rain and accompanying lightning and thunder greatly resemble a stormy night in Roswell exactly fifty years ago, Strieber remarks. The hangar resounds with thunderous cheers.

10 P.M.: Mary Pasternack, who bills herself an "intergalactic belly dancer," performs on a soaked field near the Convention and Civic Center. She has replaced Bud's Bar for this evening's entertainment. At age forty-six, Pasternack goes onstage twice a week in front of various clubs and organizations in southern New Mexico. When she isn't dancing she works as the parking director for New Mexico State University in Las Cruces. Oh, yes: Pasternack says the pointed cups of her brassiere are made of titanium—the lightest metal on Earth.

SATURDAY, JULY 5

9 A.M.: Roswell put dozens of paramedics on alert this week, but the only accidents in town have been a few fender-benders and a case or two of heat prostration. Crime is on the increase in Roswell—in March 1997 there were thirty-five shooting incidents, mostly street-gang related. But during Encounter '97 the only gun

fired was the starter's pistol at the beginning of a 5K road race—
the Alien Chase.

At the Crash and Burn Parade, held along Main Street, every
contestant, it seems, wears the aluminum foil of an alien or the
white tape of an Air Force test dummy. One man with a shaved
head is costumed in the outfit of Captain Jean-Luc Picard, the commander on *Star Trek: The Next Generation*. "Hey!" an onlooker
booms. "Telly Savalas!" The winning entry in the event is a saucer
made from an upside-down, plastic swimming pool that has been
spray-painted silver. The saucer rotates atop a bicycle-powered
apparatus. When the bike contraption reaches the judges' stand,
smoke pours forth from the saucer and it is shot heavenward—
or at least a few inches upward.

3 P.M.: Stanton Friedman is the final speaker of UFO Encounter
'97. With his raveled beard, tangled brows, and wide eyes, Friedman looks more than a bit devilish. He's met with godlike cheers,
though, particularly when he calls Roswell "the most important
story of the human race." Friedman tells of a recent poll in England in which 100,000 people were asked if they believed in
UFOs. Ninety-two percent, according to Friedman, answered in
the affirmative. "It takes courage for Roswell to stand up and say,
'This is where the space ship landed!'" A standing ovation follows.

Fortified by Friedman's words, the crowd breaks for Comedy
Night, to be held at another NMMI assembly hall. The stand-up
comedians hired for that event, apparently no Gary Shandlings
among them, beforehand go over jokes with each other to avoid
duplication.

Didja hear the one about the dummy from Roswell?
He bought some land on Venus.

Know why aliens love Roswell?

Where else can you find people who don't know how to read or write.

Know why the UFO landed in Roswell?
Because Yuma was closed.

The Encounter '97 planning committee had wanted to land Jeff Foxworthy for Comedy Night, but came up short. Like comics everywhere, Foxworthy hasn't been able to keep his hands—and lines—off Roswell:

> Perhaps you have finally decided that all the clichés about Southern families are true. You know the ones: We all marry our sisters and look for UFOs. Well, they're not true. I'm just dating my sister and I couldn't swear it *wasn't* a weather balloon.

9 P.M.: Out at Hub Corn's ranch, a music festival goes on as scheduled. Earlier in the year, the promoters of Encounter '97 had sought to hold a rock concert at the old RAAF airstrip. This would be an all-night Woodstock, with perhaps 150,000 attending. All that fell apart when the mass suicide of members of Heaven's Gate, the saucer cult, gave UFOs a bad rep and caused numerous rock stars to back away. The Corns have been advertising camping permits for ninety dollars in hopes visitors might want to sleep where the aliens landed, especially on the night of the fiftieth anniversary. But on Friday, only one person had pitched a tent.

With the big names of music bowing out, organizers scrambled to find talent at the last moment, but no stars signed on. And yet there was word at the eleventh hour that androgynous rocker David Bowie was close to coming, and his possible appearance sent a buzz through the festival crowd. To believers, Bowie is held in high esteem. After all, he played an alien in *The Man Who Fell to Earth*. And he writes and sings of galactic experiences, from 1969's enigmatic "Space Oddity" (For here am I sitting in a tin can far above the world. Planet Earth is blue and there's nothing I can do . . .) to 1972's "Starman," which truly solidified his interest in the extraterrestrial:

> Look out the window, I can see his light,
> if we can sparkle he may land tonight.
> Don't tell your poppa or he'll get us
> locked up in fright.
>
> There's a Starman waiting in the sky,
> he'd like to come and meet us,
> But he thinks he'd blow our minds.
> There's a Starman writing in the sky,
> he's told us not to blow it, 'cause
> he knows it's all worthwhile; he told me
> let the children lose it, let the children use it,
> let the children boogie.

11 P.M.: Puffing introspectively on a Tiparillo, a bread-truck driver at Bud's Bar announces knowingly that the number of UFO sightings decreases after 10:30 P.M. each night. Bud's suddenly goes quiet with thought until a patron asks that isn't 10:30 about the time when most people go to bed.

SUNDAY, JULY 6

8 A.M.: An editorial cartoon in the *Albuquerque Journal* depicts a surgeon performing an alien autopsy. As the physician removes each organ and hands it to a waiting nurse, he says, "Air Force report . . . book deal . . . bag of money . . . movie project . . . tourist bonanza . . . another Air Force report . . . another bag of money."

10 A.M.: The Wilbur Vault Company of Roswell ("The Wilbur Way") has provided a leopard-skin lined burial casket that serves as a time capsule, to be opened on the 100th anniversary of the incident. The vault sits in front of the Convention and Civic Center and visitors walk by and throw in Frisbees, beer cans, *Star Wars* figures, Danielle Steel paperbacks, recipes, letters, calendars, Dallas Cowboys posters and money. Money continues to be the unspoken language here. In this morning's *Roswell Daily Record*, the headline of an advertisement for the First National Bank of Chaves County says, "Do you feel like you're talking to an alien when you call your Roswell banker?"

NOON: Walter Haut to a correspondent from Asian News Service: "People have asked me what kind of toilet paper I used back in 1947. Damned if I know."

A barrel cactus with an alien face scratched into it rests on an abandoned table just off Main Street. A sign stuck to the cactus says, "Make an offer." In a gutter nearby lies a discarded postcard of a behemoth spaceship hovering over the Statue of Liberty. In the media room, it's reported that between two and two and one half million dollars was spent in Roswell this week. Stan Crosby is already talking another Encounter week—next year's. "We want Roswell," he says, "to be just like Capistrano."

chapter 4

Yes, We Have No Aliens

*"It was what, in the 1950s or whatever . . . ? You had that spaceship . . .
that thing that you found in New Mexico . . . Roswell . . . Roswell, New
Mexico . . . yeah . . . you had the spaceship and you had the bodies
and they're all locked up in a bunker."*
—*Independence Day*, 1996

TWO OR THREE TIMES A WEEK, perhaps, strangers will
telephone the public affairs office at Wright-Patterson Air
Force Base, in Dayton, Ohio, to ask the following sort of questions:

Where's the building at where y'all hold them space aliens?

Do you give guided tours of that flying saucer?

*My nephew says you been a-keepin' those creatures from Roswell.
Can you please tell me what they look like?*

For years UFO believers have stubbornly refused to give up on
the idea that the odds and ends recovered at Roswell in 1947
wound up at Dayton, Ohio, at what was then called Wright Field.
According to some reports, recovered objects—a craft and alien
crewmen, to be specific—were taken first to the Roswell Army
Air Field hospital, where a nurse, wild-eyed with fright, supposedly told local mortician Glenn Dennis that three "very mangled"
bodies "three to four feet high," had undergone an autopsy and
were being transported to Ohio. A military pilot who said he flew
the bodies and spaceship to Ohio swore they were not of this earth.
FBI documents show that a "disk" arrived at Wright Field at that

time, but the Air Force later said again and again that it was a top-secret weather balloon. In time the story grew, and, thanks in great measure to the media, became part of popular culture.

Indeed, the Wright-Patterson story remained so persistent and so resilient that it nearly rammed out of the way everything else, including the Ohio base's celebrated namesakes. In 1904, Dayton bicycle shop owners Orville and Wilbur Wright, hunting for a flat piece of soil on which to do some experimental flying and add to the historic lift-off they made at Kitty Hawk, North Carolina, the year before, picked a spot on an elevated plain, east of Dayton. The brothers, wearing tweed suits and bowler hats, could soon be found regularly tinkering about this prairie as they refined their power-driven, heavier-than-air-machine.

For a time, two bases—Wright Field and Patterson Field— existed near Dayton. The latter was named for a young lieutenant from the area who had been killed during a test flight. On September 18, 1947, the Air Force split with the Army to become a separate service, and the following year the two Dayton bases merged.

Today, Wright-Patterson, or Wright-Pat, as it is commonly known, is headquarters of the Air Force Materiel Command, and responsible for buying and maintaining the Air Force's warplanes and weapons. With 22,000 civilian and military personnel, down from about 31,000 during the final years of the Cold War, Wright-Pat is still Ohio's largest single-site employer. The base, divided into three, far-as-you-can-see areas, covers 8,000 acres and accounts for 1,575 buildings. In one of those buildings, it's long been deduced, lie the leftovers of Roswell.

No one is completely sure how the story got started. Of far more certainty: the Air Force has consistently denied from the beginning that any aliens or space vehicles have ever been anywhere near Wright-Patterson. In fact, the Air Force has grown considerably tired of the tales and the inquiries they bring. "Our stance," confirms Helen Kavanaugh, a Wright-Pat public affairs officer, "is

that the 'little green men' thing never happened here. We're trying to move away from that whole notion."

The idea that Wright-Patterson might be a receptable for something extraterrestrial surely had some merit in 1947, for Wright
Field at the time was the center for structural probes on all nature
of craft. It was the Army Air Force's home for technical expertise.
Moreover, the base also served as the command post of what later
became Project Blue Book, the Air Force's official investigation into
flying saucers.

Wright-Patterson has long attracted aviation scientists, including Robert H.Goddard, the rocketry genius who shot off his creations in Roswell all during the thirties. Goddard himself went to
Wright Field in 1940 to tell the military the benefits of liquid fuel
propellants as opposed to solid fuels. The once secret F-117 and
B-2 Stealth aircraft programs were linked to Wright-Patterson,
and Wright Laboratory, the nation's biggest aeronautical reasearch
complex, can also be found on the base. Part of Wright Lab's research reportedly has involved work on the hush-hush Aurora
spyplane program. If any American military installation had
knowledge of UFOs, the base would have to be Wright-Patterson.

One version of the aliens-in-the-closet story has its genesis in a
twenty-foot-long, sixty-foot-high mural that appears on a concrete
interior wall of a building in Area A of the base. The building now
is used for office space, but during World War II it was a warehouse that also served as a dining hall for German prisoners of
war. The painted wall is the only remaining sign that from 1943
to 1948 between 200 and 400 German POWs at Wright-Pat
resided there. (Coincidentally, a similar number of Germans were
interned at a POW camp south of Roswell during the war.) The
surviving mural has been restored and there is a movement under
way to have it listed on the National Register of Historic Places.
The mural features vividly colored, leering monsters with bug-
gish eyes and prominent teeth. Though demonlike, the figures,

perhaps taken from German folklore, wear amused expressions. (Another coincidence: German POWs held near Roswell were ordered to do stonework in a park close by where the annual UFO shindig takes place. The POWs fashioned an artistic German cross there that can still be observed.)

No one has ever stepped forward to take credit for the Wright-Pat mural and historic-preservation specialists say the depictions are unlike artwork found anywhere. Creation of the art, it's believed, likely served as an attempt by the prisoners to retain their cultural identity and give them a sense of solidarity. Through the years, however, the renderings have taken on another meaning, for the dominant color of the mural is green. Bruce Ashcroft, a historian formerly attached to Wright-Patterson, says that the mural pushed people to think of little green men—and off the legend roared.

The building where the aliens and spaceship have long been suspected to be stored has never been a secret. The structure stands in Area B, on Fifth Street, part of a red-brick complex that for several decades bore the name Power Plant Laboratory. Altogether there are eight buildings here, and most were constructed in the 1920s and were among the earliest Wright Field edifices. The buildings initially housed Wright Lab's dynamometers—instruments used to measure the thrust or power of engines. These days much of the work in the buildings is confined to the testing of sensors and radar detection devices.

One of those red-brick buildings—18F—gained greatest notoriety. Built in 1945, its purpose was to house the Power Plant's cold rooms. The facility had four rooms for low temperature testing of engines and accessory equipment at high altitudes. Because of the refrigerator-cold temperatures inside, for UFO enthusiasts the building took on a special deep-freeze meaning.

Building 18F eventually was named Hangar 18 by UFO conspiracy buffs, even though the massive, boxy, three-story structure could never be confused with a place in which to park an airplane or even a spaceship. Out of the woodwork—or brickwork, in this case—came proponents of that theory, however. Norma Gardner, who had worked at Wright Field in 1947 as a civilian with a top-security clearance, later announced that she had been assigned to catalog the events surrounding the Roswell incident. Gardner revealed to family and friends that she had seen two alien bodies as they were being moved to Hanger 18 and that she typed the autopsy reports that listed the beings as standing four to five feet tall and having large heads and slanted eyes.

Telephone calls to Wright-Patterson asking about Gardner's claim or someone else's haven't always come from the United States. When *Project UFO,* produced and narrated by Jack Webb, appeared on British television in the late 1970s, Wright-Pat's public affairs office received a cascade of overseas inquiries from viewers of a show that was later voted by critics as among the worst science fiction ever to sputter across a TV screen.

In time, Hangar/Building 18 was accorded distinguished status by the media, which of course only perpetuated the Roswell link. One of the first big events to catapult the hangar's fame was Charles Berlitz and William L.Moore's *The Roswell Incident,* the 1980 work that mentioned at length Wright-Patterson's connection to Roswell. The book quotes Norma Gardner on her deathbed, rationalizing her testimony about what went on in Wright-Pat's top-secret area: "Uncle Sam can't do anything to me when I'm in my grave." The same year that *The Roswell Incident* came out, Hollywood released the movie titled *Hangar 18.* Promotional copy for the film offered these teasing questions:

> What would happen if a UFO were to crash land on
> Earth?
> Would the government let us know?
> Or would they fear nationwide panic and keep it under
> cover?

The plot of *Hangar 18* has the U.S. space shuttle, in the midst of deploying a satellite, colliding with an unidentified flying object. The UFO makes a crippled but safe landing in the Southwest, where it is swiftly carted away by government agencies to an Air Force base, to a secret Hangar 18. Operated by NASA as a lunar landing reception area, Hangar 18 has the usual decontamination chambers and biological labs.

It should go without saying that *Hangar 18* did not receive any Academy Award nominations. The movie featured astronauts with mop-top haircuts and pot bellies, a spaceship whose interior mirrored a Las Vegas casino, and aliens who bore an uncanny resemblance to the Addams's Family character known as Uncle Festus.

Repeatedly, the movie's cover-up theme borrows lines that have for years been associated with Roswell. Robert Vaughn, portraying an oily presidential aide out to do all he can to reelect his boss, snarls to underlings at various times the following:

> "Keep the lid on Hangar 18."

> "We've got to keep this thing bottled up."

> "We keep everything buttoned down."

Hangar 18's UFO, it turns out, did not crash in New Mexico, but in fictitious Bannon County, Arizona, which could pass for New Mexico and certainly looks more like New Mexico than the much later Showtime movie *Roswell*, which depicted flapjack-flat Roswell as being rimmed by mountains. (It's unclear whether Bannon County, Arizona, is located near Piedmont, Arizona, where a plague-bearing U.S. satellite went down in Robert Crichton's 1969 thriller *The Andromeda Strain*, an early literary provacateur of Roswell recollection.)

In any event, Bannon County sits in the desert, making *Hangar 18* hold fast to popular culture's Desert Dictum. Roswell-originated, and stoked by dozens of science-fiction movies of the 1950s, that law says that when spaceships crash, they must go down in the desert—as happened in Roswell. An appendage to the Desert Dictum, the Double-Wide Statute was added in the 1980s to include trailer courts as crash sites, after *Uforia*, a funky 1981 movie about a UFO cult—far less horrifying than the Heaven's Gate group of 1997 that committed mass suicide—took place mostly in a mobile home park in the desert. Like tornadoes, flying saucers appear innately attracted to prefabricated homes.

During the fifties, according to many accounts, UFOs regularly smacked into lonely dunes or barren mesas. In *Aboard a Flying Saucer*, a best-selling non-fiction book in the early 1950s, Truman Bethurum, a heavy equipment operator, told of napping in his truck between shifts one night in the Nevada desert. Awakened by the sound of people talking, when Bethurum sat up he said he was startled to find his pickup completely surrounded by eight small men who seemed to be of Latin extraction. They took him to their nearby flying saucer, said Bethurum, where he met the captain, a stunning blonde woman named Aura Rhanes, who told Bethurum she was from the planet Clarion.

The Desert Dictum works as a law because if a UFO lands in barren wasteland, there is a good likelihood that no one will see it land, which is the point of the law. Similarly, vacant Sonoran terrain represents much more mystery as a landing site than, say, a block of high-rise apartments. For example, in 1953's *It Came From Outer Space*, the first 3-D science-fiction movie made, a leathery old telephone lineman, a guy who has spent his life on the high poles of the Southwest, waxes philosophical about the tricks that empty, dry lands can play on a person, particularly someone who says he has just spotted a flying saucer heading into the ground:

> After you've been working out on the desert fifteen years
> like I have, you hear a lot of things. See a lot of things

too. Sun in the sky. The heat. All that sand out there. Sometimes rivers and lakes that aren't real. And you think the wind gets in the wires and hums and listens.

In *Hangar 18*, it's an airport maintenance man working in the arid nothingness who addresses why the landscape might make a fella think he's seen a UFO:

"It's the desert air that does it."
"Does what?"
"Dries out your brain juice so's you can't think no more."

Close Encounters of the Third Kind appears an exception to the Desert Dictum, for the mother ship in that 1977 movie plops down near Devil's Tower National Monument. There are, however, no exceptions to the fashioning of popular culture principles. Devil's Tower may sit in northeastern Wyoming, but it also stands at the exact longitude of the Roswell crash site. Just as curious are co-incidences by way of a footnote: Steven Spielberg, director of *Close Encounters*, was born in 1947 and as a kid lived in Phoenix—in the desert.

The astronaut heroes of *Hangar 18* finally stumble upon the spot where the ship nosed in—a dusty arroyo featuring a circle of scorched ground, all hidden from view by scrub cedar branches. Talk about a cover-up! Soon the astronauts are being pursued by two men in dark suits and driving a dark Lincoln, obviously early-day Men in Black.

The spaceship of *Hangar 18* has a great deal in common with accounts of Roswell's ship, particularly in the hieroglyphic-like symbols on the console, markings that greatly resemble the ones remembered in 1947 by Jesse Marcel Sr., the Roswell Army Air Field intelligence officer.

"Whaddya think?" asks Darren McGavin, a good guy NASA functionary who employs the same gravelly, grilling tone he used in the early 1970s on television's *Kolchak, the Nightstalker*, a poor man's *The X-Files*. McGavin here is quizzing a *Hangar 18* technician about the meaning of the spaceship's assortment of dials and screens and the strange writing on the dashboard.

"Well," says the technician after a few seconds pause, "they sure didn't get this equipment at RadioShack."

The debut of *Hangar 18* caused a fair amount of stress to the telephone switchboard operator at Wright-Patterson Air Force Base. These days, when the What-have-you-done-with-the-aliens? calls to the Ohio base come in bunches, Helen Kavanaugh remembers to check the television listings in the newspaper to see if by chance *Hangar 18* had just been shown on some late-night cable network, where it sometimes appears under the title *Invasion Force*, and with an entirely different ending.

Odd thing about hangars: ever since Roswell, UFO addicts love them like chocolate. In *The Doomsday Conspiracy*, writer Sidney Sheldon's 1991 thriller about a spaceship that has smashed into the Swiss Alps, the remains of the crash are kept at Virginia's Langley Air Force Base, inside a sealed chamber, inside—*Hangar 17*. The two aliens retrieved in *The Doomsday Experience*—a third alien is strolling around and posing as an Earthling—undergo an autopsy in the hangar, a scene that barely predated *Alien Autopsy: Fact or Fiction?*, a 1995 headline-grabbing television program.

The banquet that came near the end of Roswell's week-long UFO Encounter '97 celebration was held, by popular demand, at the old RAAF base, inside Hangar 84, where some people are sure that in 1947 aliens and a ship were stashed aboard a C-54, which then headed for Wright Field. Others now contend that Hangar 84 wasn't the right hangar at all, that the real one at Roswell is no more.

Frank Scully's controversial book *Behind the Flying Saucers*, which appeared to great clamor in 1950, was one of the first places to mention Wright Field as being the storage spot for flying disks and alien cadavers. Sixteen years later, John Fuller's book *Incident at Exeter* added more details. A best-seller during the days when sightings were blamed on everything from bad eyesight to bad gas, *Incident at Exeter* recounts how a house-sized saucer is seen by a cluster of people in a New Hampshire small town. Fuller writes:

> There have been, I learned, after I started the research, frequent and continual rumors (and they are only rumors) that in a morgue at Wright-Patterson Field, Dayton, Ohio, lie the bodies of a half dozen or so small humanoid corpses, measuring not more than four and a half feet in height, evidence of one of the few times an extraterrestrial spaceship has allowed itself either to fail or otherwise fall into the clutches of the semi-civilized Earth people.

A novel titled *The Fortec Conspiracy* did nearly as much to churn the Dayton-Roswell rumor mill as *Hangar 18*. Written by Richard M. Garvin and Edmond G. Addeo, and published in 1969, the book was a wild story about Wright-Patterson's Foreign Technology Division, which does indeed exist as a testing center. In the novel, Fortec is a super-secret inner sanctum where it is rumored that three aliens, recovered from a crashed saucer in Norway, were being kept like pickled kosher dills.

Barney Russom, the novel's hero, believes the reported suicide of his twin brother, a researcher at Fortec, has something to do with the downed saucer story. A friend tries to tell him otherwise: "The Air Force, Barney, is on *our* side . . . I would be ashamed to think that our government would ever consider withholding such information. . . ."

With those words, Russom is off and sniffing like a Roswell bloodhound. In a short space of time, Russom digs up his brother's grave, finds another man's body in the casket, breaks into Fortec, swipes one of the aliens, wraps it in a blanket and puts it into a station wagon, drives to a small airplane, hops in with the alien in tow, and then flies away. Russom is going to tell the world what the Air Force won't. A cross-country chase ensues, lots of people die, and the alien, it turns out, has a deadly virus that spreads like chicken pox.

A constant proponent of the Wright-Pat's-Hiding-Something Theory was Leonard Stringfield, a chemical company public relations man from Cincinnati. A former pilot who said he first saw a UFO during World War II, Stringfield became the first mainstream ufologist to declare crash/retrieval reports a matter of legitimate concern, even vital interest. Stringfield, who died in 1994, published his hallmark *Situation Red, the UFO Siege!* in 1977, and with it came overnight fame. He gave workshops everywhere, edited a UFO newsletter, taught the first college-accredited UFO course in the country, and every night stood in his Ohio back yard with binoculars in hand and searched the skies. And always, Stringfield dripped paranoia: he claimed his phones had been tapped, which he took as reassurance that he was on to something.

Stringfield reported that a crashed saucer fifty-feet in diamater and containing humanoid bodies was taken to Wright-Patterson in 1952. He writes, "Until the 1970s, the little creatures were more amusing to UFO research than a subject meriting serious study. Official agencies scoffed at the charge they were hiding twelve refrigerated little men at Wright-Patterson AFB."

But Stringfield felt otherwise; he was convinced that Wright-Patterson possessed a secret hangar. After a while, the Stringfield Theorem, which it shall now be known, made it essential for any UFO researcher to mention the following items when referring to the contents of a suspected hangar: tarpulins or crates to conceal the alien bodies; blocks of ice—always *dry* ice—to maintain those bodies.

During the 1980s, Stringfield published his own tracts, which were filled with accounts from unnamed sources or from people who had heard them from someone who knew someone else who had worked at Wright-Pat some years before. In a 1989 booklet titled *UFO Crash Retrievals: Is the Coverup Lid Lifting?*, Stringfield talks of a man who saw five crates on a forklift inside a hangar at Wright-Pat. In each of these crates, Stringfield reports, were the recovered dead bodies of small humanoids—from Arizona. Another Stringfield story involved four bodies, five feet in height, that were kept in a deep freeze morgue at Wright-Pat, kept at approximately 120 degrees below zero. Roswell, of course, captivated Stringfield. American astronaut Ellison Onizuka reportedly told Stringfield that in 1973 he had seen a black-and-white movie at McClellan Air Force Base in Alabama that showed alien bodies from Roswell "on a slab." Stringfield liked to recount the testimony of a woman whose father had told her he stood outside a hangar—at the Roswell base where a wrecked saucer was kept—and peeked under a tarp in the back of a truck. "He saw two small dead bodies . . . they looked yellowish and a bit Asian."

When Stringfield refused to identify his sources, the skeptical latched onto a line from *Hangar 18*: "If you want to show that the Air Force is concealing a flying saucer, you've got to have substantial proof, or you're just another nut."

TV's *Unsolved Mysteries* in 1990 added another log to the Dayton/Wright-Pat fire. A 1995 broadcast of *Sightings*, a nationally syndicated show about the paranormal, gave the Dayton chapter ten minutes. *Sightings* featured an interview with people who had relatives who had said "we have all the bodies from the crash." Leonard Stringfield tells the interviewer, "They had thirty alien bodies at Wright Field alone up until 1966." At last count, as many as forty saucers and more than 100 alien cadavers are stored in North America, according to John Spence's *World Atlas of UFOs*, published in 1991. *UFO Crash at Roswell*, by Kevin D. Randle and Donald R. Schmitt, and the book's sequel, labor to tie Roswell to Dayton. The authors say the craft, "twenty to twenty-five feet long, and fifteen to twenty feet wide, was more of an angular craft, more of a lifting body, not the classic domed dish. It was more like a space-shuttle configuration. Clearly it was not a balloon." Randle

has subsequently explained that technicians at Wright Field spent three weeks crawling through every inch of the recovered space-ship, which had "basinette-like" seats.

As well as being a ufologically rich part of the United States, Ohio has long been a leader in outer-space news. The state is, after all, the home of John Glenn, the first American astronaut in orbit, and Neil Armstrong, the first American on the moon. Space travel, of course, seldom is discussed without mentioning saucer travel. Armstrong, according to Len Stringfield, reportedly spotted an un-identified craft while making his historic lunar landing in 1969. (Armstrong has firmly refused to comment.) In terms of UFO news, Ohio may rank second to New Mexico. Wright-Patterson for sev-eral years was home to Project Blue Book, the Air Force organi-zation that kept track and investigated all UFO sightings. (Project Blue Book never makes mention of the Roswell incident, which meanwhile gives UFO followers paroxysms.) J. Allen Hynek, a dis-tinguished UFO researcher who coined the term "close encounter," began his astronomy career in Columbus, the same city where a large radio telescope, Big Ear, earned a mention on *The X-Files*.

For many years Ohio has stood among the top ten states in re-porting glimpses of UFOs. Stringfield explained that fact this way: "There is something that triggers intensive UFO surveillance, something that is undetected by human sensors." Eddie Ricken-backer, the World War I flying ace and a Ohio native, believed in flying saucers, and the state's former governor, John Gilligan, said he saw a saucer while in office. The people who spotted oblong objects over northeast Ohio in 1973 won a $5,000 award from the *National Enquirer* for the most "scientifically valuable" discov-ery. The Lake Erie region of Ohio averages fifteen sightings a year, and one theory has it that there's an underwater passage for UFOs that runs between Lake Erie and Niagara Falls.

Many telephone inquiries to law enforcement officials in Ohio ("You people seen that big UFO tonight?") have turned out to in-volve the Goodyear blimp, which is headquartered in Akron. A

Blockbuster video store blimp floating over mid-Ohio in 1995 generated more than 100 anxious phone calls.

Prior to the Wright-Patterson saga, the biggest UFO story in Ohio took place at the same time as the Roswell incident. In fact, some researchers say the Circleville, Ohio, incident clearly reinforces the belief that a weather balloon fell near Roswell. It seems that Circleville's Sherman Campbell had gone to the local sheriff with what he thought was the solution to the mystery of flying disks that had been seen around the country in June and July 1947. On July 5, 1947, Campbell found a strange item on his farm. On July 6, newspapers nationwide ran a photograph of Campbell's daughter Jean holding what appeared to be a kitelike piece of a balloon. No one in Ohio thought the find was anything but a balloon, and the incident was mostly forgotten. The Roswell balloon story, of course, was not forgotten, at least by the Air Force. These days, Circleville, located twenty miles south of Columbus, is famous for an annual event similar in scope to Roswell's yearly UFO extravaganza. Circleville's celebrity has nothing to do with UFOs, and yet it draws scads of fans just the same. In fact, the community's Pumpkin Festival each fall attracts an estimated 400,000 people.

The legend of Wright-Patterson refuses to leave, for, seemingly, no one wants it to go away. In 1992, a politician running for office in California, announced apropos to nothing that Wright-Patterson definitely had the aliens. "They are short, stout beings. They are very powerful. They can leave upon their own wish and they choose not," said Kip Lee of Redding, California. The beings, Lee added, were kept in a basement. Trouble is, responded Wright-Pat's public affairs office, there exists no basement on the base. No Hangar 18, no basement, not even a "Blue Room," a secret lab likely named for Project Blue Book, according to a few earnest researchers.

Meanwhile, UFO protectors have used any means to keep the Wright-Patterson story alive, including the promotion of this sur-

vival technique: Holding Onto the Casual Remark. Some time in the 1970s, U.S. Senator Barry Goldwater reportedly cornered General Curtis E. LeMay, former chief of staff of the Air Force. LeMay had been a good friend of Colonel William Blanchard, the commander of the RAAF in 1947 and the officer who ordered the famed press release written that said the Army had recovered a flying disk near Roswell. LeMay also was a pal of Blanchard's boss, General Roger Ramey who, some conspiracy speculators say, switched the Roswell saucer story with one about a real weather balloon.

"General LeMay," Goldwater was said to have casually remarked, "what do you have there at Wright-Patterson that's so top secret we can't see it?"

Supposedly, LeMay grimaced, then answered, "Don't *ever* mention that again."

LeMay's reply, which surely can be taken various ways, has long served UFO adherents as indication that the Air Force did indeed have something at the base—something alien. Holding Onto the Casual Remark occurred again in the seventies when astronaut Gordon Cooper, appearing on *The Merv Griffin Show*, said he had heard the U.S. government was actually able to keep a few UFO occupant crash victims alive for several days. If any housewives were ambivalent about UFOs, the esteemed anthropologist Margaret Mead may have helped to change their minds in a *Redbook* magazine article in September 1974. Offering readers more than a casual remark to hold onto, Mead flatly stated that UFOs existed. Finally, UFO diggers latched onto a remark made by Arthur E. Exon, a retired general who, in July 1947 was a lieutenant colonel stationed at Wright Field. In words that are regarded by believers as sacred as the Sermon on the Mount, Exon remembered the piece of material coming in from Roswell that July and said all sorts of tests were done on it. "The overall consensus," said Exon, "was that the pieces were from space."

By the time the movie *Independence Day* premiered in 1996, popular culture was done with casual-remark games. It was now time to play show-and-tell. In fact, the movie shows the recovered spaceship from Roswell and three insect-like aliens. Two aliens, the movie tells audiences, had died in the crash, the other a few weeks later. Trouble is, *Independence Day* had kept the aliens not at Wright-Patterson, but at Area 51, the government's ultra-covert saucer garage in Nevada.

Anthropologist Benson Saler calls the Roswell incident a modern myth, a story that many people say they believe because, well, that's what they've always believed. In truth, myths involving flying saucers are nothing new. As long ago as the 1940s Swiss psychologist Carl Jung was theorizing about the myths behind what we think we see in the skies. Saler and colleague Charles Ziegler, who along with Charles Moore in 1997 authored *UFO Crash at Roswell: The Genesis of a Modern Myth*, came up with six versions of the Roswell myth and they say that authors of books on Roswell are like collectors of folklore. The Wright-Patterson story can't truly be labeled a myth, however. It has more qualities of what Jan Harold Brunvand calls an urban legend. Brunvand, who teaches folklore at the University of Utah, has tracked many well-known urban legends such as the "The Kentucky Fried Rat," about the woman who discovered that her take-out chicken was actually a batter-fried rodent. Brunvand is interested in modern urban legends, those bizarre but believable stories about spiders in hairdos and Cabbage Patch dolls that receive funerals.

Storytellers, says Brunvand, usually believe that their accounts are true, and many legends have appeared in print or on television as genuine news stories. But the same basic tales have been circulating for years—"Only their details change as they are adapted to the local fast-food restaurant, lovers' lane or discount store." Brunvand theorizes that urban legends can survive in our culture as living narrative folklore if they contain three essential elements: a strong basic story appeal; a foundation in actual belief; a meaningful message or "moral."

Though he isn't acquainted with the Wright-Patterson legend as such, Brunvand knows well "The Landed Martians," an urban legend with all three essential elements. According to Brunvand, supposedly a UFO from Mars, with a number of humanoid creatures aboard, crashed in the Midwest many years ago. U.S. Air Force personnel recovered part of the craft and its occupants, one or two of them still alive, before the rest of the spacecraft was destroyed in the resulting fire and explosion. The remaining UFO parts and the "creatures" were moved to an isolated hangar in the desert of Arizona or Texas or New Mexico, and the men involved in the action were sworn to secrecy or lied to about the nature of their mission. Various "documents" alleged to be based on interviews with these men that piece together the true story circulate among UFO and science-fiction buffs from time to time. Indeed, *Newsweek* reported in 1983 that a group called Citizens Against UFO Secrecy had filed a petition in U.S. district court in Virginia demanding release of "one or more occupants of crash-landed UFOs of apparent extraterrestrial origin." The occupants were described as "three-foot tall, humanlike creatures wrapped in fine metallic cloth."

The role of the automobile in many well-known urban legends is significant, Brunvand relates. As tellers of American urban legends, whether adolescent or adult, "We are a highly mobile and often affluent folk, so it is natural many of our favorite plots involve private cars and public roads." Two automobile stories—involving trucks, in both cases—have in recent years propped up further the Roswell/Wright-Patterson story. The first tale involves Jim Ragsdale, who came forward in 1994 to say that on July 4, 1947, he was necking with his girfriend in the bed of his pickup in a remote mountainous location near Roswell when a UFO crashed nearby. Ragsdale's depiction fits Brunvand's "lovers' lane" criterion, a subplot of nearly every B science-fiction movie of the 1950s.

Roswell apparently has a way of making people come clean before they die. Forty-odd years after the fact, Ragsdale made a deathbed confession, just as Norma Gardner had done. Ragsdale admitted he had drunk a lot of beer that summer night in 1947 and that he was "buck nekkid" in the back of his truck when the UFO "come through the trees fifty yards away." Ragsdale said that he and his girlfriend went to the site and found little aliens and a spaceship outfitted with tiny "thrones" and a bejeweled instrument panel. The couple, said Ragsdale, then fled before military personnel arrived.

The Day After Roswell, published in 1997, refines the Stringfield Theorem and adds an annotation. In July 1947, Philip A. Corso, the book's author, was a young Army officer stationed at Fort Riley, Kansas. Corso said he was running a security check at the base one night when an enlisted man suddenly motioned him over to a warehouse. A few days earlier, according to Corso, five large Army trucks with trailers attached had convoyed to Fort Riley from Fort Bliss, Texas. The trucks were stopping in Kansas on their way to Wright Field and the Air Materiel Command. The trucks' cargo was being temporarily stored on the base, before continuing on to Ohio, though Corso doesn't explain why. Inside the warehouse, Corso peeked at one of thirty wooden crates on the convoy. Inside one crate he saw a four-foot figure with human looking features, but obviously not human. Years afterward Corso realized what the cargo had been and decided that the United States government had used the Rowell spaceship to increase technology by "back-engineering" the foreign vessel.

While Wright-Patterson's public affairs office these days continues to field telephone calls about aliens, no longer are television crews allowed to stand in front of the base's Building 18F and record, with a knowing grin, sound bites for the evening news. Print reporters who show up at Wright-Pat eager for a UFO take are encouraged to seek more legitimate stories on the base.

It's never been easy for outsiders to crack Wright-Patterson, no matter what the subject is. When American rocket scientist Robert Goddard went to Wright Field's Experimental Engineering Station in 1940 to obtain funding for his launches, the Air Force turned a deaf ear. Goddard's wife Esther later said that the trip to Ohio served to "harden her husband's misgivings about the military's politics and influence in the granting of contracts." Of course, by July 1943 the Army had established a rocket proving ground at White Sands, New Mexico, to build a two-step rocket, as Goddard had advocated, and to use a German V-2 as the first stage.

The handsome, sprawling United States Air Force Museum, which stands adjacent to Wright-Patterson, certainly doesn't have a welcome mat down for those visitors interested in UFOs. A tiny cabinet that sits almost as an afterthought on the second floor is the only sign of extraterrestrials in the place, a fact that further supports the Air Force's attempt to distance itself from the topic. The museum's little display case mentions that when Project Blue Book, formerly called Project Sign and also Project Grudge, closed at the end of 1969, the act formally ended the Air Force's involvement with flying saucer matters. Project Blue Book, which operated out of Wright-Patterson beginning in 1953, was strictly an outgrowth of the Cold War and the paranoia that swirled about the saucer sightings of 1947. One of the project's early directors, Captain Edward Ruppelt, coined the term "UFO." Between 1947, when Project Blue Book began, and 1969, it investigated 12,618 sightings. Of that total, 11,917 were found to have been caused by material objects (balloons, satellites, and aircraft); immaterial objects (lightning, reflections, and other natural phenomena); astronomical objects (stars, planets, the sun and the moon); and weather conditions and hoaxes. Seven hundred and one sightings remained unexplained. Roswell never appeared in Blue Book because the military changed its mind and declared the flying disk retrieved there really was a weather balloon.

Project Blue Book finally was halted because no UFO reported, investigated, and evaulated by the Air Force had ever given any indication of threat to national security, and there was no evidence that any sightings were extraterrestrial. Conspiracy fans like to remind people that the acclaimed J. Allen Hynek quit Blue Book because he allegedly said the project's strongest cases were going to a secret, higher-up program.

The United States Air Force Museum's UFO display case contains only about a dozen or so items. On one shelf rests a clear shiny object about the size of a thumb. An accompanying note card reports that object fell from the sky and struck a farmer's tractor near Corpus Christi, Texas, in 1962. When the farmer, who was plowing a field at the time, climbed down from his tractor to pick up the object, it burned his hand. The farmer took the piece to authorities who eventually sent it to Wright-Patterson where it underwent extensive tests by Project Blue Book researchers. Part of a spaceship? Not at all, analysts finally determined. The object was a hunk of glass, apparently made by the Libby-Owens Company, of Alton, Illinois.

As Dayton's story of cryogenically-cupboarded aliens persisted, in 1994 U.S.Congressman Steve Schiff of New Mexico asked the General Accounting Office, which is the investigative arm of Congress, and the Air Force to search all files for Roswell-related documents. The first answer, which didn't touch much on Wright-Patterson, came in 1995, when the Air Force identified the object found in Roswell as part of "Project Mogul," an exotic-looking, top-secret balloon built to acoustically monitor Russian nuclear bomb tests and ballistic missile launches. The Mogul explanation didn't dent the urban legend. In fact, it only served to keep it fresh, for the cover-up folks refused to believe for a minute the balloon story, one the Air Force had kept coming back with for almost five decades. The Air Force's final word came in 1997's *The Roswell Report: Case Closed*, a narrower version, particularly in physical heft, of the Air Force's exhaustive, doorstoplike 1995 study,

The Roswell Report: Fact Vs. Fiction in the New Mexico Desert. In the foreward to *Case Closed*, Sheila E. Widnall, Secretary of the Air Force, sounds like a former student of Jan Harold Brunvand. Widnall writes, "The Roswell incident has assumed a central place in American folklore."

The 231-page *Case Closed* advances the notion that a balloon accident at Roswell's Walker Air Force Base in 1959 figured prominently in the Roswell-Dayton scenario. It seems that a Captain Dan B. Fulgham, based at Wright-Patterson, had been on assignment to New Mexico. Fulgham was participating in a high-altitude balloon flight near Roswell when his balloon and its 900-pound aluminum gondola crashed and pinned him. Struck by the gondola, Fulgham suffered a severe head injury. His head swelled so much, observers said he looked like a "blob." When Fulgham was taken to Walker, a few people got their first view of his distended cranium, sunken and puffed-closed eyes and yellow skin. *Case Closed* says: "A witness claimed he had seen a 'creature' walk under its own power in the hospital . . . the injury caused Fulgham's head to swell, resembling the classic science-fiction alien head." With his eyes almost closed shut and a turban of bandages around his head, when Fulgham got off the plane at Wright-Pat, his wife shrieked, for she failed to recognize him. Rumors apparently quickly spread that the Air Force had retrieved a live monster from outer space.

Fulgham's story sparked new interest in the Roswell crash, which the Air Force eventually said involved another balloon—this one carrying research dummies. The Air Force suggested that this event, like the crash dummies and a slew of other circumstances, got twisted around in people's minds and created a mirage that spiraled alien invasion theories and inadvertently made Fulgham a noted figure in flying saucerdom. An enlarged head with slits for eyes and wrapped in a white cloth might resemble, well, an alien.

Fulgham, in a 1997 interview, said, "I never heard anyone say I was an alien until the Air Force talked to me. People have always speculated about other life forms from space and my accident just threw gas on their alien fire. I hate to ruin the stories, but as far as I can tell, I'm not an alien from outer space. If I was, maybe I'd have a better golf game."

So the legend lives on and the telephone calls to Wright-Patterson keep coming:

Remember those railroad tracks that were down near Highway 263 on the base? Well, they were hauling a UFO along those tracks and my grandpa told me the top of that flying saucer come off. Somebody took pictures of it, Grandpa swears. It was in all the newspapers. You got any of those pictures left?

Rob Young, a historian for the National Air and Intelligence Center, a Wright-Pat building that used to house Project Blue Book, says, "One guy threatened to have me arrested if I didn't release the aliens." Young works in a building that has a utility tunnel running beneath the length of it. He says that callers are sure that tunnel is where the Roswell aliens are kept. Bruce Ashcroft, Young's predecessor, once did an "electronic search" of several million pages of Wright-Patterson documents, in Ohio and at the Air Force's Historical Research Agency in Alabama. Ashcroft was hunting for one word, a single reference to perhaps "aliens" or "saucers." He found nothing.

What about that teevee show the other night, the series called JAG? It had them aliens being kept in some warehouse . . . Where's that warehouse at?

These days, when a person calls Wright-Pat to report a UFO, he or she is advised to contact a private or professional organization interested in aerial phenomena, and a list is provided. If a caller feels his public safety is endangered by a UFO, he's encouraged to contact a law enforcement agency. If the caller asks about secreted space aliens, the base public affairs office responds by sending out a sheet of paper with these words in large bold letters:

There are not now,
nor have there ever been, any extraterrestrial
visitors or equipment on
Wright-Patterson Air Force Base.

For many people, those words are still not enough.

chapter 5

A Couple of Cans of Worms

*"This man knows our most intimate secrets from the last half century:
the alien-landing at Roswell . . . the truth about the JFK assassination."*
—*The Rock*, 1996

THESE DAYS, ROSWELL'S STATURE in ufology needs no hard-sell to maintain. The town's name-brand recognition does most of the marketing, with little outside help. In the past, however, matters extraterrestrial anywhere have required large amounts of assistance to gain public approval, and the publication of two Roswell-fed books shouldered much of that load. Though neither *Behind the Flying Saucers*, which appeared in 1950, nor *Communion*, which came along in 1987, was *about* Roswell, both best-selling books expanded awareness of the New Mexico incident and made lasting—albeit controversial—impressions on how Americans view UFOs.

Francis Joseph Xavier Scully, a convivial, New York-bred Irishman, had been looking for a subject to write a book about for a couple of years when he stumbled onto flying saucers in the late 1940s. Because Scully was a wise-cracking columnist for *Daily Variety*, the show business tabloid, flying saucers would seem a little unusual for him. But Scully had his serious side: for most of his adult life he had been an invalid. He had lost a lung to tuberculosis and a leg to shrapnel in World War I. He suffered from constant pain of osteomyelitis and spent a great deal of time on his back. He rarely complained, however, and in jest he named his California home "Bedside Manor."

Almost no books had been written about flying saucers until 1950, though several were reported to be in the works due to the recent string of unidentified sightings. Early in 1950, Bernard Newman published a novel, *Flying Saucer*. Among other things, it told of a flying disk that affected automobile ignitions. Newman's book created a minor stir after several reports suddenly surfaced of flying disks that had mysteriously killed car engines.

On the coattails of Newman's work, Donald Keyhoe spun out *The Flying Saucers Are Real*. Keyhoe, a former Marine pilot, was convinced the Air Force was hiding downed saucers from the public, a view that would later make Roswell famous but in 1950 didn't provide the necessary cachet. Unlike many Roswell researchers, Keyhoe did not offer proof of a landing or a crash to make his book take off. The book chiefly was an interpretation of data and theories. A large section focused on the death of Air Force pilot Thomas Mantell, whose F-51 jet fighter went down under mysterious circumstances in Kentucky on January 7, 1948. Mantell's last words from the cockpit to the tower today read as if they've been taken from a 1950s movie: "I've sighted this thing! . . . It looks metallic and it's tremendous in size! . . . I'll try to close in."

Minutes later, Mantell's fighter disintegrated with tremendous force and it was Keyhoe's belief that Mantell had died while chasing a flying saucer. *The Flying Saucers Are Real* might be completely forgotten today if the book's jacket, illustrated with a glittering, egg-shaped spaceship, had not been turned into a hot-selling poster.

Then came Frank Scully. Scully had met Silas Newton, an oil prospector and raconteur, in the mid-1940s and quickly grew impressed, particularly with the man's gift of gab. In September 1949, Newton introduced Scully to Leo GeBauer. Though GeBauer had been a land speculator, Newton referred to him only as "Dr. Gee," a geophysicist who allegedly was an expert in magnetic research. GeBauer had done "top-secret work" for the government, including, reportedly, the inspection of a crashed disk at Roswell. He was also involved first-hand in the retrieval of a UFO that went down at Aztec, New Mexico, about 450 miles northwest of Roswell, an accident that GeBauer attributed to the craft's "magneto trouble."

Without bothering to check out either Newton or GeBauer, Scully began to write columns for *Variety* about the Aztec incident. The columns triggered remarks by nationally syndicated columnists Dorothy Kilgallen and Walter Winchell, which in turn fanned a flame under Scully to do something in a hurry.

Scully's agent found a reputable publisher, Henry Holt, and in seventy-two days Scully cranked out *Behind the Flying Saucers*. On September 6, 1950 the non-fiction work, running 230 pages, was published to great fanfare. The cover illustration was nothing short of attention-getting. A drawing showed a group of fearful-looking people cowering and pointing at the sky. The jacket blurb said, *The book everyone is talking about. Behind the Flying Saucers*, which detailed the Aztec crash and the work of Dr. Gee, strongly influenced the contactee movement, and it spawned the rumor of crashed UFOs and dead occupants for decades to come. Aztec's resemblance to Roswell, occurring only a little more than two years before, but well-known in the intelligence community and through newspaper accounts, was uncanny. From its descriptions of a flying saucer with a metallic skin no one could damage, to little bodies being retrieved; from accusations of an Air Force cover-up to the whisking away of materials to Wright Field in Ohio, the subject matter of *Behind the Flying Saucers* bore a striking likeness to the 1947 incident in southeast New Mexico.

Strange but true: Roswell may have fathered Aztec, but Aztec gave birth to Roswell. Elements of Aztec—including hieroglyphic symbols on the control panel and scraps of metal saved from the spaceship—are thought to be catalysts for other crashed flying saucer stories, including the Roswell incident, in which long-hidden souvenirs of the vessel are still turning up years later.

The Aztec event generated good grist for the publicity mill, just as Roswell would do afterward. At the same time that Scully was considering a book, Mikel Conrad, a Hollywood actor/producer/director was releasing a movie titled *The Flying Saucer*. To bolster his film, Conrad held a press conference in the fall of 1949 and said he had footage of a real saucer taking off and doing tricks in the air. The announcement made headlines across the country and, goaded further by Newton, the event pushed Scully into action. In a *Variety* column Scully said he and no one else was privy to all there was to know about flying saucers and told of a trip he made to the Mojave Desert with Newton and Dr. Gee to demonstrate magneto research. When the Air Force Office of Special Investigation interviewed Conrad, he confessed that he had invented the whole story. Scully, however, with Newton still giving him "inside" information, had clearly made his decision that aliens had landed.

The frankness of *Behind the Flying Saucers* touched young and old. *Weekly Reader*, the magazine for grade-school kids, boldly reported in its September 18–22, 1950 issue: "Flying saucers are made in several sizes. The smallest ones are twenty inches in diameter. They are six inches thick. The big ones are about as far across as the widths of four or five city lots." A widely circulated comic book *Vic Torry and His Flying Saucer*, appeared in the fall of 1950. Test pilot Vic Torry and his aviation enthusiast girlfriend Laura are trying out an X-3, a new jet plane, over southern California. Suddenly, a strange disk appears—and heeding the Desert Dictum, lands in the Mojave. Vic and Laura decide to take a look. The couple learns that the crew of aliens is from Mercury, a planet that apparently is plagued by internal strife. To correct things, Vic and Laura fly the crippled saucer back to Mercury where they're able to bring peace.

Inspired by Frank Scully's words, Charles Duffy in 1950 penned a hit song, "I'm Looking for Flying Saucers in the Sky":

Whenever I go outside I start looking high and wide,
I'm looking for flying saucers in the sky—
Not a soul I want to meet as I'm walking down the street,
I'm looking for flying saucers in the sky.
Now people think I'm high-hat or maybe in a daze,
But there's one thing they don't know that I've got the
    saucer craze.

I want to see those saucers flying through the Milky Way,
I'm looking for flying saucers in the sky.

The roots of the Aztec story remain unclear. Though numerous witnesses came forward to talk about Roswell years afterward, George Bowra, a longtime newspaper editor in Aztec, later interviewed more than 100 people—cowboys, ranchers, lawmen—who lived or had spent time in the area. Bowra could find no one who remembered a flying saucer going down. However, just as Roswell had experienced a military aircraft accident almost a decade after its incident (a KC-97 tanker crashed in 1956, killing eleven Air Force members), a P-38, a World War II-era fighter plane, had ditched on a highway east of Aztec because of engine trouble, around 1948. People who lived in the area remembered that the plane sat for about a week until the military came in and disassembled the craft and trucked it out. A few residents in Aztec vaguely recalled a newspaper item that joked about a nearby crash of a flying saucer. Somehow, that joke worked its way up to Denver, where George Koehler, a radio station announcer, picked it up and put on the air that alien bodies and the remains of two saucers had been found near the southwest Colorado border. The three-foot-tall humanoids came from Venus, said Koehler, and their ship was powered by magnetism. Silas Newton, who lived in Denver, was listening to that broadcast, for he and Koehler were friends. In March 1950 Koehler helped bring Newton to Denver University to give a lecture on flying saucers. During that talk, Newton mentioned his scientist friend, Dr. Gee, who had been asked by the military to examine three crashed saucers, including one at Aztec, and sixteen alien bodies in all. At Newton's urging, Frank Scully attended the lecture and subsequent news of it spurred Scully to begin immediately on *Behind the Flying Saucers*.

Scully's book, which wove saucer history around the Aztec incident, was not short on eyebrow-raising text. The first saucers, Scully said, were equipped with toilets and berths because the pilot thought the duration of the trip would require them. Later saucers cancelled the commodes—because the pilot learned how quickly the trip could be completed. The saucer from Venus that landed in Aztec came here because the crew was curious about atomic explosions in the South Pacific. Dissection of the Aztec cadavers, Scully said he'd been told by Dr. Gee, revealed that there was no blood, but rather a liquid smelling similar to ozone. The bodies had no digestive tract, but perfect teeth. Of greatest importance, as far as Roswell is concerned, is that Aztec aliens were as gray as March ice.

Portions of *Behind the Flying Saucers,* particularly those dealing with science, sound as if they were taken directly from the hit television show of the time, *Captain Video*. Scully noted, for example, that the saucer utilized a "magnetron oscillaton cyclotron frequency." The speed at which *Behind the Flying Saucers* was written showed: the book was padded with newspaper accounts of sightings, and contained numerous typographical errors and blatant mistakes. For instance, Pluto was said to be the nearest planet to the sun. Despite such carelessness, *Behind the Flying Saucers*, priced at $2.75, sold more than 30,000 hardbound copies. *Pageant* magazine ran a condensed version, which further boosted sales.

Although Scully announced that he had never actually seen a

flying saucer in person, UFO buffs immediately embraced him. Scully was a lively writer, for one, a quality lacking in the flying saucer field. Moreover, a major New York publisher had handled his book, the first work of its kind to get such treatment, and that gave the project great credence. "You are our first hard-cover press agent," a woman reader rejoiced. Scully responded by thumping his own tub. He traveled to Chicago to plug the book, and along with the UFO magazine *Saucerian*, he hosted a well-publicized party in that city. He dropped hints that Warner Brothers and Walt Disney had shown interest in a movie.

Even bad notices didn't hurt sales. *Behind the Flying Saucers* was reviewed everywhere, and seldom flatteringly. The *Chicago Tribune* said, "If compelled at pistol point to make the choice, this reviewer would recommend the work as fit reading only for children but never for adults beyond the fairy tale level of intelligence." "Scully's science," said *Time*, "ranks below comic books." Many critics thought the work was a spoof. After all, Scully had once penned a comical little treatise titled *Fun in Bed*. Syndicated columnist Bob Considine wrote, "Now I understand why Jules Verne sold well and why the New Jersey farmers (as depicted in Orson Welles's radio version of *The War of the Worlds*) stampeded in terror."

Ignoring the barbs, Scully basked in the book's success. Meanwhile, stories began to circulate that there was something very wrong with *Behind the Flying Saucers* besides poor proofreading and twisted physics. In 1949, Ken Purdy, then editor of *True* magazine, had tried to get Scully to write the Aztec story for his publication, for $3,000, but Scully had turned Purdy down. *True* later came out with two damning articles about the Aztec incident, and *The Saturday Review of Literature* delivered its own debunking story. All three pieces claimed Scully had been part of a scam perpetuated by Newton and GeBauer, veteran bunco artists, according to the articles. J.P. Cahn in *True* said, "The whole story was as phony as a headwaiter's smile." Indeed, a shard of metal that Newton said came from the Aztec crash proved after testing to be nothing more than a substance used in pots and pans, a tale echoed years later in Roswell.

The issue of fraud broke wide open in October 1952 when Newton and GeBauer were indicted in Denver District Court on two counts of conspiracy to commit a confidence game swindle involving oil well exploration tests and electronic "doodlebugs." One of these devices was represented as costing $800,000 when in truth it was a war surplus item worth less than four dollars. The two men had been able to close the shady deal by spring-boarding the fame they had gained through Scully's book. After a month-long trial in late 1953, Newton and GeBauer were convicted, given suspended sentences, and ordered to make restitution. Newton later became embroiled in worthless stock transactions tied to a Utah uranium mine. After Newton's death in 1972, there were no fewer than 140 claims filed against his estate by people Newton had "borrowed" money from to exploit various oil or mining claims. GeBauer, hounded afterward by a series of lawsuits centered around a questionable Arizona real estate deal, died in 1982. He hadn't spent a day doing "top-secret" government tasks.

Behind the Flying Saucers never did make it to the big screen. However, the "GeeBee" race plane, featured in the Walt Disney film *The Rocketeer* (1991), came straight from the Scully affair.

Though mired in disputation, Scully's book did not stop the nation's hunger for flying saucer news nor did it halt the mass media from nourishing that hunger, particularly through the printed word. Indeed, the country suddenly felt an extraterrestrial explosion, beginning with the Popular Books reprint of *Behind the Flying Saucers*, in 1951. *The Coming of the Saucers*, by Kenneth Arnold and Ray Palmer, came out in 1952 with this promise: "No trickery, no practical jokes, no 'top secret' . . . the only book that tells the whole truth and nothing but the truth." Donald Keyhoe, the former Marine pilot, was heard from again, in 1952, with *Flying Saucers From Outer Space*. Subtlety no longer ruled when book publishers dealt with the extraterrestrial. On the front of *Flying Saucers From Outer Space* was a big bold arrow that said, "Important, See Back of Jacket." On the back was a letter from a Department of Defense official that read, "The Air Force has never denied that this possibility (of flying saucers) exists . . . if the apparently controlled maneuvers reported by many competent observers are correct, then the only remaining explanation is interplanetary travel."

The following year, another much ballyhooed book, *Flying Saucers Have Landed*, by George Adamski, appeared. Adamski, who had little formal education and had worked as a maintenance man at Yellowstone National Park, referred to himself as "Professor." Adamski wrote that he had had an experience with an alien—in the desert, naturally—near Parker, Arizona, in 1947, a pivotal year for flying saucers. The alien he met, said Adamski, was an average-sized man with flowing blond hair, a deep tan, perfect teeth, calm green eyes, a one-piece brown suit and sandals. Adamski said the alien gave him a ride in his saucer and told him, by communicating through sign language, that he was concerned about this planet's atomic radiation. In the fuss over the book, no one apparently noticed that only two years before, an alien expressed the same concern in the popular movie, *The Day the Earth Stood Still*.

Rocket scientist Daniel W. Fry apparently had also seen *The Day the Earth Stood Still* as well as read about the Roswell incident, for in Fry's *The White Sands Incident*, published in 1953, the author revealed how he had witnessed a UFO landing on July 4, 1950—in the New Mexico desert. The alien in Fry's book, a casually-dressed, white male named A-lan, told Fry he was trying to "help you people on Earth alter the present flow of events and avert a holocaust which is otherwise inevitable."

Not everything about flying saucers was so foreboding. The romance of space travel received a shot in the arm through the 1954 pop song "Fly Me to the Moon." That same year the Hamilton Watch Company ran full-page advertisements in magazines announcing a new timepiece that would tell the time on Earth and Mars simultaneously. A *Time* magazine cartoon in 1954 showed a young woman, out stargazing one night, suddenly being tugged toward a spaceship by aliens. The caption: "Come on—we'll show you our moon." The pulp magazines *Fate* and *Point* regularly ran articles about saucers through the 1950s. *Point* even published a purported legitimate photograph of a twenty-seven-inch-tall alien who had supposedly survived the crash of a flying disk near Mexico City. News reports that year gave much space to Harold T. Wilkins who argued that the recent crash of a British jetliner had been caused by flying saucers, which, Wilkins said, had been observing Earth for 1200 years.

Rumors, often a big part of any UFO argument, circulated regularly through this period. The wildest story concerned President Dwight Eisenhower. UFO believers were certain that Ike signed a secret exchange treaty that would swap aliens with Americans who wanted to trade places. Frank Scully, who had been quiet at first during attacks on his book, now defended himself, which only kept UFOs in the public eye. In 1957, Scully appeared on *The Tonight Show*. "Like girls," Scully told host Jack Paar, "flying saucers are here to stay."

Just as things were about to die down, the eminent psychologist and philosopher Carl Gustav Jung published *Flying Saucers: A Modern Myth of Things Seen in the Skies*, in 1958. The book was something of a departure for an intellectual, though Jung explained he had become interested in the subject in 1946 and had started collecting data on it soon after. "I am not qualified to contribute anything useful to the question of the physical reality of UFOs," Jung wrote. Only the "psychic" aspects concerned him. Most surprising was the praise Jung gave two other books, both fiction, published in 1957: *The Midwich Cuckoos*, by John Wyndham, and *The Black Cloud* by Fred Hoyle.

Wyndham's novel concerned a presumably extraterrestrial being that casts a spell on a remote English village. The spell causes residents to go to sleep and kids to awake with golden eyes. The book later became the smash-hit movie *The Village of the Damned*. Hoyle's *The Black Cloud* told of a dark cloud of gas that is drifting toward our solar system, causing many to believe that the formation is an invasion of Earth by star-dwellers.

As earnest as some people now began to look at flying saucers, UFOs still revealed an absurd side, particularly as the Cold War wound down. In 1961, a Wisconsin farmer reported that he had come upon three creatures standing beside a UFO. The three, the farmer said, were wearing black turtlenecks and knit helmets, and they were cooking *pancakes*.

Just when the Scully saga began to fade, it reemerged in 1986 with the publication of *UFO Crash at Aztec: A Well Kept Secret*. William Steinman, a metallurgist from California, had read *Behind the Flying Saucers* in 1981 and had become convinced that unscrupulous journalists had blindsided Scully and dishonored the good names of Newton and GeBauer. Scratching at every conceivable piece of the Aztec incident, Steinman turned out a 625-page tome, the author's first writing project. Steinman described at length the existence of a powerful, highly select group of professionals—military and scienfitic—who ordered the entire town of Aztec under close scrutiny. "Their phone calls, all mail and all movements were monitored at all times. All their relatives, schoolmates, teachers, close friends, etc., were also watched like a hawk. This close surveillance is still going on thirty-nine years after the event, and will continue until MJ-12 sees fit to relax the net." The MJ-12, a UFO auditing group, also known as the "Majestic 12," had been in force since the late 1940s, conspiracy theorists believed. Included in the crash recovery team, according to Steinman, was the godfather of the atomic bomb, J. Robert Oppenheimer. William E. Jones, a respected UFO researcher from Ohio, wrote in 1991 that "Neither the Scully book nor the Steinman book is persuasive." Jones had spent months trying to find someone in Aztec who had knowledge of the crash, but, like George Bowra years before, could not locate anyone. Indeed, Jones thought the Aztec crash might have been a smokescreen to avert attention away from the *real* crash of a UFO, the one that occurred in Roswell.

While at work at his typewriter in Palm Springs, California, in June 1964 Frank Scully suffered a heart attack and died. He was seventy-two. Friends had urged him to write a sequel to *Behind the Flying Saucers*, but Scully had declined. The subject had become a bore, he replied. Still, favorable mail concerning the book was being forwarded to Scully two years after his death. To the end, Scully argued that what he had written was true, that a saucer had crashed. "I took a lot of kidding about the book . . . the biggest laughs came from the report that the flying saucers were piloted by small men. I asked, if people believed Mickey Rooney was real, why did they think men from outer space had to be giants? I finally dismissed the subject by saying, 'Maybe they sent down their jockeys. After all, it was a long trip and in long rides weight makes a lot of difference.'"

It seems likely that Scully was a victim, not a perpetrator, of a hoax. However, one still must wonder: Bernard Newman's 1950 novel *Flying Saucer* had to do with chicanery concocted by a scientist *and* a writer. In *The Image: A Guide to Pseudo-Events in America*, Daniel Boorstin says, "We have become eager accessories to the great hoaxes of the age. These are the hoaxes we play on ourselves." Many call *Behind the Flying Saucers* one of the grand publishing deceptions of all time, and rank it with the Hitler diaries and Howard Hughes's autobiography. The fraudulent nature of the book surely damaged Scully's journalistic reputation and his output afterward suffered. Some UFO researchers refuse even to deal with the Aztec incident—Kevin Randle and Donald Schmitt in *The UFO Crash at Roswell* and its follow-up, *The Truth About the UFO Crash at Roswell*, give the Scully episode only a few paragraphs. And yet for others, the Aztec story is still revered. Upon the fiftieth anniversary of that story, Aztec townspeople, realizing how well Roswell had profited, celebrated their own UFO festival. In terms of money made, the Aztec party was not nearly as successful as Roswell's. But then all Aztec officials wanted to do was take in enough to help the public library buy a few dozen new books.

Meanwhile, Frank Scully lives on—in a way that would surely bring amusement to the witty show-business columnist. When Chris Carter, creator of *The X-Files*, wondered what to call one of his program's extraterrestrial investigators, a role that would be played by actress Gillian Anderson, Carter, long a student of UFOs, eventually came up with the same last name as the author of the first major best-seller on the subject.

For many cultural historians, Scully's book reverberated the ruse accomplished by Phineas T. Barnum's "Fejee Mermaid." In 1842, Barnum put a stuffed creature on display at his New York City museum and announced it was an actual mermaid. To publicize the attraction, Barnum circulated 10,000 pamphlets on New York City streets advertising her appearance and in the first week thousands of people came to get a glimpse.

If the mermaid wasn't real, it was the niftiest fabrication anyone had ever seen—an ingenious sewing together of a large fish's body and tail to the head, shoulders, arms and rather pendulous breasts of a female orangutan.

The mermaid bore no real obvious marks of artifice, though Barnum sensed it was a fraud when he received it. Curiously, Barnum, who knew every crowd had a silver lining, apparently felt guilty about this contrivance, much more so than his "Wooly Horse," a normal equine with cotton glued on. Barnum eventually admitted that his "wonder of creation" was in reality nothing but a taxidermist's handiwork. He pulled it from his museum, and to the end of his life Barnum would say he was "not proud" of the entire incident.

Coincidentally, pictures of Barnum's mermaid viewed today resemble some people's description of an alien.

So what does an alien really look like? Frank Scully said the little men found at Aztec were three and a half feet tall, had large slanting eyes, diminished noses, spindly bodies, long arms and webbed fingers. That humanoid description, advanced in the movies *E.T., The Extraterrestrial* and *Close Encounters of the Third Kind*, was truly sharpened with the publication of Whitley Strieber's *Communion*, which made an almond-eyed, pointy-chinned face as recognizable as any head on Mount Rushmore.

A Texan born in 1945, Strieber spent his early career in New York City, where he worked for several advertising agencies. Later, he became a freelance writer of science fiction and horror stories. On December 26, 1985, Strieber said he was sleeping with his family at their cabin in upstate New York when small visitors suddenly whisked him away to their vessel, stuck a needle into his brain and eventually returned him to his bed. The event, which Strieber decided later had happened to him on other occasions, put, he said, his marriage in peril and drove him nearly to suicide. Only by writing about it was he able to feel a sense of relief. The resultant book, published by William Morrow & Co, quickly rose to No. 1 on *The New York Times* bestseller list in 1987, and remained there for months.

Strieber's story, like Scully's, was well-written, though not particularly new. According to the *UFO Encyclopedia*, in 1912 on an island off Scotland called, improbably, Muck, two children were accosted on a beach by small people dressed in green who, said the children, spoke English and Gaelic and cast a spell. Through the years, little green men have given way to little gray ones. Little aliens for a time gave way to six-foot-tall pale blonde beings. There have been herky-jerky robots and vicious monsters and enough dripping, entomological sub-species to keep *Alien* sequels going well into the twenty-first century.

So what does an alien really look like?

Orson Welles's radio broadcast of *The War of the Worlds* in

1938 gave America a Martian few listeners could imagine more terrifying:

Having tentacles and a body as large as a bear; it glistened like wet leather, eyes black and gleaming like a serpent, a V-shaped mouth with saliva dripping from rimless lips that quivered and pulsated.

Bug-eyed oafs from deep space were still stumbling about in the 1950s, even though Frank Scully said Venusians looked a lot like grade-schoolers. The fifties were a time of creatures in the movies. These things usually grabbed the girl in their claws and didn't let go until the screaming ceased. They ran the gamut, these fiends, from a giant paper spider (*Cat Women of the Moon*, 1954), to zombies in silk pajamas (*Plan 9 From Outer Space*, 1956), to horticultural horrors (*Invasion of the Star Creatures*, 1963). Those aliens brought a certain comfort and viewers giggled at them, knowing that nothing could actually look like that. This nonsensical notion was personified in the 1958 hit song "Purple People Eater":

Well, I saw the thing a-comin'
out of the sky, it had one long horn
and one big eye—
I commenced to shakin' and I said,

Ooh-wee—it looks like a purple
people eater to me.
It was a one-eyed, one-horned,
flyin' purple people eater . . .

To reach the status of *Communion*, an alien simply had to become more recognizable, and that evolution began. Television's

Outer Limits in the 1960s featured giant ants with hideous human, Roswell-like faces: protruding eyes, oversized heads, and disproportionate arms. A *Twilight Zone* show in the sixties featured a beautiful woman alien banished from her planet because the rest of her race resembled pigs. Even *Star Trek* didn't have creatures each week. The *Enterprise* encountered planets full of Indians, gangsters from the 1920s, Nazis, and ancient Romans. The metamorphosis truly took off with *Close Encounters* in the late seventies and *E.T.* in the early eighties, though the *E.T.* alien was more of a turtle without a shell and seemed derived from a number of sources, including Yoda, the green-skinned Jedi warrior of *The Empire Strikes Back* (1980). By the 1990s, and the movie *The Arrival* (1996), human-like aliens had been given a special touch: they walked backward.

To the contactee, the humanoid alien's color and physical characteristics have been all-consuming. Mack Brazel suggested the bodies in the Roswell crash were as gray as gunmetal. That color was seconded by Grady L. "Barney" Barnett, an engineer for the U.S. Soil Conservation Service. "The heads were round, the eyes were small, and they had no hair," said Barnett. "The eyes were oddly spaced." The 1995 docudrama *Alien Autopsy: Fact or Fiction?* showed alleged footage from an autopsy following the Roswell crash, and the bodies were definitely gray. But as the late U.S. Representative Steve Schiff, who spent a year of taxpayers' time and money burrowing into the Roswell incident, said because the film was black and white, the alien's color was uncertain. Then Schiff added words that are key to understanding how popular culture becomes a part of us: "It (the body) was humanoid, as they say in the science-fiction movies."

A Roswell Army Air Field nurse allegedly told witness Glenn Dennis in 1947 that the bodies in the base hospital were "little beings, with large flexible heads and concave eyes and noses." But when one is recalling an alien, descriptions change like the seasons. The authors of the *The Roswell Incident*, the initial study on the subject, said the bodies appeared to be male. And yet the *Alien Autopsy* cadaver definitely looks to be female. Tim Good, author of *Above Top Secret*, wrote of a woman whose father had said he stood outside a hangar at Roswell where the saucer was stored and saw "two small dead bodies . . . they look yellowish . . . a bit Asian." *Popular Mechanics* magazine resurrected that idea in its July 1997 issue by theorizing that the Roswell aliens, because of their eyes, might have been Japanese, sent to the U.S. after the war. If true, they were far better behaved than that other postwar Nippon export, *Godzilla*.

Writing in *The New Yorker* in 1997, Kurt Andersen said of humanoids, "Those wan, innocent naked creatures appeared during the Woodstock era and after, supplanted the scheming, sinister superhuman aliens typical of the anti-communist fifties." *Communion* defined that popular conception. In fact, Strieber welded everything from Scully to Roswell to Barney and Betty Hill's celebrated abduction experience in 1961, which Strieber admitted he had read about extensively, to construct an alien that seemed to spring from the same corner of the national psyche that worships Walter Keane's paintings of grotesquely doe-eyed children. With Strieber's input, artist Ted Jacobs did the memorable cover of *Communion*. Jacobs's celebrated illustration, which became as startling as the front of *Behind the Flying Saucers*, reappeared on the Avon Books edition in 1988 and thus wound up at every airport newstand from Adelaide to Zurich.

Here was a humanoid, four and a half feet tall, with a large hairless cranium, flat nose, small ears set lower than a human head, and coal-black, teardrop eyes that looked like the slots from a gumball machine. "By far the most arresting feature in this face was the eyes," said Strieber. The eyes of an alien are *always* important. In *Alien Autopsy: Fact or Fiction?* a pathologist is seen peeling the irises off the alleged extraterrestrial cadaver. The physician surely was following the same procedure used by actor David Bowie to remove his cat-like eyes in *The Man Who Fell to Earth*.

Buying into an alien today is like buying into cigarettes: none of them is really good for you, of course, but the buying—and the smoking—goes on. What's more, a consumer gets his choice: colossal grasshoppers (*Starship Troopers*, 1997), gloppy reptiles (*Alien*, 1979), or a sexy, reconfigured squid-woman (*Species*, 1995). And when a consumer wants something ordinary, something packaged without pizzazz, he can plunk down money for the offspring of the *Communion* alien, a thing with a plain old utilitarian face, seized and trademarked by Roswell and almost everywhere else now, it seems. Meet the Generic Alien.

Like *Behind the Flying Saucers*, *Communion* did not go down well with critics, many of whom accused Strieber of creating the story. Thomas M. Disch in *The Nation* devoted eight pages of castigation to *Communion*, and argued that as a horror novelist Strieber knew "all kinds of ways to make the implausible seem plausible." An article in *Publishers Weekly* called the book a "deplorable trend in publishing" and questioned whether *Communion* ought to be marketed as non-fiction, even though the book was subtitled "A True Story."

Strieber countered, just as Scully had done, by making it known that he had received hundreds of supportive letters from readers. Like Scully, Strieber went public to defend his book, on *The Tonight Show* and *Phil Donahue*. *Report on Communion*, written in 1989 by Strieber friend Ed Conroy, and issued by Strieber's publisher, offered, not surprisingly, a sympathetic portrait of Strieber's tribulations and came, also no surprise, with a cover illustration of an alien's face. In Roswell, few have questioned Strieber's story. After all, Strieber is held in high regard there, as anyone would be who not only set the mold for the cash cow Generic Alien, but wrote a novel about the Roswell incident. Titled *Majestic*, Strieber's 1989 book focused on a handful of sinister government operatives who inspect the UFO wreckage and then report back to President Harry Truman as he paces the White House floor in nightclothes. On the book's cover, the prevailing alien lies sprawled in an arroyo.

Fictional works have given Roswell a wider audience still. In Lee K. Abbott's O'Henry Award-winning short story "The Talk Talked between Worms," from a 1996 issue of *The Georgia Review,* the trauma of having witnessed the Roswell crash and having touched a surviving alien drives a New Mexico rancher to the loony bin. In *The Roswell Crewman,* published in 1997, author Donald Burleson writes of a surviving alien, hidden away at Holloman Air Force Base in Alamogordo, where he has spent a half-century designing electrical gizmos. The chief character in *Roswell High,* a 1998 series of paperbacks by Melinda Metz, is a young student named Max whose parents died in the 1947 crash and left him, apparently, with the ability to forever remain a mysterious teenager.

Following *Communion,* Strieber publicly hoped that the encounters that had changed his life had ended. He was wrong. The extraterrestrials came again and, of course, Strieber wrote about them, in 1988's *Transformation: The Breakthrough.* Though it drew a fair-sized following, *Transformation* did not sell as well as *Communion,* and the reason likely lay in the book's jacket. *Transformation* featured a blue-eyed alien head on the cover, but only half a head. Strieber rectified that in 1995, when he published *Breakthrough: The Next Step,* which featured on the front a full-faced alien and the familiar black, stringbean-shaped eyes.

Strieber, as one might suspect, has inspired a legion of imitators, all of whom have publishers obviously aware of the power of a dust jacket. When Budd Hopkins's book *Intruders: The Incredible Visitations at Copley Woods* appeared in 1987, the cover illustration was of woodland cottages bathed in a glowing night light. A year later, for the paperback version of *Intruders,* the cover featured an alien's head, with dark, slanted eyes and ashen skin. When Hopkins's next book, *Witnessed: The True Story of the Brooklyn Bridge Abductions,* was released in 1997, no bridge decorated the cover; only the familiar alien face. The cadaver from Fox-TV's *The Alien Autopsy: Fact or Fiction?* looked a great deal like a Whitley Strieber model; no real shock since the film seemed in perfect condition after turning up five decades later. Indeed, the cover of Strieber's book pops up briefly in the movie *Alien Autopsy*. When *Time* magazine made Roswell its cover story for the June 23, 1997 issue, the portrait on the front looked positively Strieberish, though more human than the alien face of *Communion*. In the immortal words of Pogo, "We has met the enemy, and it is us."

Certainly *Communion* had years of abduction and contactee literature to draw from, going back to George Adamski or, at least to 1954 when actor Peter Graves was snatched in *Killers From Space*. More recently, *The Andreasson Affair*, a 1979 book by Raymond Fowler that documented how several three-foot-tall humanoids entered Betty Andreasson's home in Ashburnham, Massachusetts, and then subjected her to a physical examination, had gained a wide following.

The Andreasson Affair succeeded because it did not break three requirements, call them the Abduction Axioms, that had been set down in books in the early 1950s and that have generally been adhered to since the aftermath of Roswell: the alien leader must have a name; the abductee must be physically probed, but otherwise returned home unharmed; and the abductor must declare that the mission is one of benevolence.

Betty Andreasson was delivered back to her Bay State home in one piece, but not before she said she underwent a probe of her nose and navel by the visitors' leader known as Quazguaa. "We have come to help the human race," Quazguaa told Andreasson.

The incident occurred in 1967, said Andreasson, and she at first wrote to the *National Enquirer*, which was offering big money for the best UFO tale. When the tabloid turned her down, Andreasson eventually hooked up with UFO investigator Fowler and a national best-seller was born.

The creatures, according to Betty Andreasson, "were all identical, except the leader who appeared taller. They had large over-sized pear-shaped heads. Their heads were mongoloid in appearance. They had holes for noses and ears, fixed scarlike mouths, three digit hands."

Digit counting within the UFO community has become almost as important as spaceship sighting. The Martians in the movie production of *The War of the Worlds* reveal three long fingers, the tips of which resemble the ends of toy arrows, à la some accounts of Roswell. The star of *E.T.* was considered to have set the standard, for he had three fingers and a thumb. Strieber said his visitors had four fingers—two long, with the same kind of bulblike suction tip, as seen in Roswell, and two short. The cadaver in *Alien Autopsy* shows six digits on its hands and feet. Stanton Friedman, who has made a good living out of studying the Roswell case, says with confidence that the aliens there had four long fingers.

Numbers of fingers aside, What does an alien really look like?

In truth, many theorists, and Strieber has to be among them—want aliens to look like ourselves. There's immense satisfaction in that wish, to be sure. That's exactly what Frank Kauffman, who claimed he was an eyewitness to the Roswell incident, likely had in mind when he described to *Newsweek* in 1997 the Roswell aliens he had seen fifty years before. "They were," said Kauffman, "very good-looking people."

chapter 6

Science Fiction's Godfather

"Is Roswell, N.M., the real capital of the United States? And if so, should science fiction be held responsible?"
—*The New York Times*, 1998

IN AN UNPRETENTIOUS, white clapboard house in Portales, New Mexico, across the street from a plot of peanuts—the chief crop ninety miles from Roswell—a stooped, gentle-speaking figure with a flap of white hair and prominent ears, lives by himself.

John Stewart Williamson moved to Portales in 1947, three days before the Roswell incident. A struggling writer, he took a temporary job as wire editor of the Portales *News-Tribune*. Williamson had grown up in the area, on the Llano Estacado, or "staked plains," the dry and arid region of eastern New Mexico that includes the alleged crash site in Roswell.

Jack Williamson has since become a legend in the field of science-fiction literature. He has authored more than seventy books that have been published in more than fifteen languages, as well as more than 100 short stories. He coined the terms *humanoid*, *android*, *genetic engineering*, and *terraforming*. Years ago he received a fan letter from a young Isaac Asimov, and in 1994 his name was given to a newly discovered asteroid. Twice president of the Science Fiction Writers of America (1978 and 1979), the second recipient of that organization's Grand Master Nebula Award for lifetime achievement, and the winner of a prestigious Hugo Award, Williamson, born in 1908, is a trailblazer who continues to produce. His great output has helped to push science fiction from a cramped darkened corner to the center stage of popular fiction. Today, some bookstores carry only science fiction.

The year 1947 was a significant one for Roswell as well as for Williamson. He got married that August to Blanche Slaten Harp (who died in an automobile accident in 1985), and he published his first book, *The Legion of Space*. Later, he taught English at Eastern New Mexico University, where he is now, in his early nineties, a professor emeritus and where he still teaches one course each spring. Portales holds Williamson dear. Eastern New Mexico University renamed a liberal arts building in his honor, and the town's public library has devoted a wing to him and filled it with his science-fiction writings and papers.

Literary critic Leslie Fiedler said that the period following World War II and the detonation of the atomic bomb caused science-fiction writers to feel their genre had lost its aura. However, the sudden interest in flying saucers in 1947, and in Roswell in particular, followed by the launching of Sputnik a decade later, and then the years of space exploration that followed, gave creators of science fiction a wide range of new subject matter.

Key to all of this is 1947, but not simply for the sudden flurry of flying saucer sightings that year. Rather, 1947 stands out for a lesser-known event, but one of significance in terms of popular culture. Raymond Palmer published that year in his magazine *Amazing Stories* a story about fiendish alien beings controlling life on Earth through the use of rays. Thousands of readers believed that story was true. After the war, when a paper shortage ended, pulp magazines began to flourish and continued to do so through the fifties. Hollywood tripped over itself to grind out sci-fi films, many on a shoestring. Science-fiction books zoomed off the presses.

This hunger continued through the 1960s, even as the number of pulp magazines fell back. Now it was television's turn to start a new wave, and TV helped to introduce large groups of young readers to the world of what-if. Indeed, in 1969, when police arrested cult leader Charles Manson for his part in some ritualistic murders, the only book found in Manson's possession was science-fiction writer Robert A. Heinlein's *Stranger in a Strange Land*, about a Martian who arrives to teach mankind to accept peaceful Martian ways.

Through all these eras, Jack Williamson has endured and stood out. Curiously, because of his broad knowledge of science and his proximity to Roswell—it's located southwest of Portales, down U.S. 70, a road locals call the "Roswell Highway"—and because he also once lived and worked in Roswell, one would think that Williamson would be asked regularly about the UFO incident said to have occurred in the adjacent county. Such is not the case. In fact, Williamson says he's hardly ever asked about Roswell, despite the fact that he has some surprising things to say about it.

Q: Do you believe a UFO crashed at Roswell?

A: I suppose most people think that all science-fiction writers *are* believers. But I don't know any science-fiction writers who *do* believe. I think Roswell is an interesting cultural phenomenon, like the Flying Dutchman or the Loch Ness Monster. It's another example of people who believe in anything. But there's no scientific basis to believe that aliens ever landed there.

Q: A colleague of yours, Charles L. Harness, thinks that as long as Roswell isn't totally debunked science fiction can continue to flourish. Harness says that when reality rears its ugly head, fantasy weeps and fades away. Do you agree?

A: To a point, yes. Certainly Roswell events have helped science fiction grow, given it a wider audience, for science fiction surely took off after World War II. But in terms of Roswell helping writers? That happens only if you're writing about creatures, about aliens who come from another world to live and walk among us.

Q: You lived in Portales when the incident occurred. Any recollections of it?

A: Not really. Oh, I don't doubt that something fell out of the sky. A high-altitude glider or a parachute maybe.

Q: Ever been to the crash site?

A: I didn't go to Roswell much as a young man. And I had no reason to go there on the fiftieth anniversary. I'm not sure I know where the site is. TV and the newspapers gave me enough. People made a lot of money off that; it was commercially a big success. But people are people. I'm interested in people; I've spent my life writing about them—as a spectator and an observer.

Q: Harlan Ellison, another colleague of yours, is terribly critical of Roswell, particularly because on the very day we landed a robot on Mars after two decades of preparation, people in southeast New Mexico were, Ellison said, buying hot dogs and saucer souvenirs and looking around for space garbage in a rancher's field. Any thoughts?

A: [*Laughs.*] It takes all kinds, I suppose. Most of what we know about Mars has already been put into books. But you know some of those books, take the Mars one by Edgar Rice Burroughs, they didn't do very well after NASA sent its Viking probes to Mars in 1976. What's interesting to me is that the photos of Mars look a great deal like the landscape of New Mexico. By the way, in the early 1950s, I wrote a syndicated comic strip for a while that originated in the New York *Daily News*. It was called *Beyond Mars*. Still, the two things happening at the same time—landing on Mars and celebrating Roswell—do put things into perspective. It makes you pause to consider what truly is important.

Q: You've been extremely prolific, but you've never written about bug-eyed monsters from space. Instead, your work often concerns some form of futuristic machinery, presented, well, in a rational, thoughtful manner. Didn't you ever get the urge to write about UFOs?

A: What I did in 1950 was suggested by all the clamor of flying saucers, including, I would guess, Roswell. I worked out a fictional scenario in which secret and superior observers could really be watching us. I doubt that all the odds of evolution would create anything resembling us. To make my watchers human, I assumed them to be cousins of ours, descendants of people who left the prehistoric Earth to escape the old catastrophe that refilled the dry Mediterranean and erased all traces of their origins here.

Q: Was this ever a book?

A: I sold a series of shorts and novelettes about these astronauts, who have achieved their own galactic civilization and returned to shelter our own fumbling progress. In 1962 the stories were collected in a paperback called *The Trial of Terra*.

Q: The term *humanoid*, which you're credited with inventing, is used repeatedly when referring to the aliens supposedly recovered at Roswell. How does that make you feel?

A: I've read that in paperbacks given to me by friends who are believers. Of course, my use of it was in reference to robots, virtually omnipotent beings whose sole objective was to serve humankind. They really came to the fore at the end of World War II when we all realized that science and technology could become tools for terrible destruction. The people in Roswell, I think, are using the term to mean sort of a small person. The world is full of people who are severely convinced that the government is try-

123

ing to cover up those aliens, those humanoids. But covering up "little green men" for fifty years? It doesn't make any sense.

Q: John W. Campbell, a well-known editor of science-fiction magazines and once a mentor of yours, wrote a famous story called "Who Goes There?" It was later made into a 1951 movie titled *The Thing From Another World*, about a flying saucer that crashes into a polar ice cap. *The Thing* was one of the first flying saucer movies. There's a creature on board in the movie, a super being, who later comes unfrozen and seeks out victims. Campbell surely must have believed in UFOs?

A: In the sense of creating a story, yes. But don't forget, Hollywood changed his story some for that movie. They jazzed it up quite a bit, which they've been known to do.

Q: Astronomer Clyde Tombaugh, who discovered Pluto, said he saw something strange in the skies one night while standing in his back yard in Las Cruces in 1949. And in 1951, three Texas Tech professors saw what has become known as the "Lubbock Lights," a sensational parade of objects in the sky that remains a puzzle to this day. All of these people were well-educated. How do you explain that?

A: If I'm not mistaken, Tombaugh later said his sighting surely had to do with atmospheric reflection. And the Lubbock lights, as I recall, were determined by most scientists to be a flock of birds.

Q: Still, you must care about UFOs?

A: I think it would be tremendously interesting if intelligent beings were here. I've looked into it enough and I think it's likely life would evolve on other planets. If you consider the millions and billions of planets, then some would involve intelligent life. They might want to communicate and they might not.

Q: Then it sounds as if you believe the odds of aliens coming here or even communicating are remote.

A: Well, it would take a highly developed culture to come here and it would take a pretty selective evolutionary approach to come here. Intelligent and technical societies require an unlikely set of coincidences. The odds of another evolution being perfectly in sync with ours would be astronomically long.

Q: Suppose aliens could come to Earth . . . Where might they be from?

A: There are 250 billion stars in our galaxy and at least 100 billion in other galaxies. But we haven't discovered any other planets beyond our solar system. We still haven't found another sun with a solar system like ours.

Q: Then we're talking of going beyond our solar system. That's pretty far, isn't it?

A: The distances then would be vast. We're simply too far apart. The distances between stars are enormous, making interstellar journeys extremely remote. When you consider that light travels 186,000 miles per second, it would take four years to reach the nearest star. It would take light 100,000 years to cross the galaxy and two million years to reach the nearest neighboring galaxy, the Andromeda galaxy. To visit a planet 200 light years away, you would have to travel 1200 *trillion* miles. That's a fair distance, I'm afraid. When *Voyager* was launched, it was the fastest machine ever set forth from Earth and it traveled at only one ten-thousandth the speed of light.

Q: And yet if they could make that trip . . . ?

A: Our bodies are oxygen and nitrogen and carbon and hydrogen and some of these compounds can be observed in molecular clouds in space. The chemicals of life can fit themselves together. But if you look at the record of geology, life on Earth is four and one-half million years old, and there is no evidence anybody was here before. There's no record that any conquerors came here. Our geologic record shows the Earth's evolving species all grew on the same planetary family tree, all akin, never supplanted by space invaders.

Q: Earlier you suggested a glider or a parachute might be responsible for Roswell.

A: I think something was picked up there. It could have been the wreckage of a balloon sent by the Japanese. Those mainly landed during the war and afterward in the Northwest, where they started fires. Maybe this one just took longer to travel and the government got nervous because the United States is always supposed to be invincible. I've simply considered what could have fallen out of the skies.

Q: During the war, you were stationed at Roswell Army Air Field. What were you doing there?

A: I was a weather observer, at the beginning of 1943, for six months in Roswell. I was a staff sergeant. I was mainly on the ground, plotting weather maps, reading weather instruments and sending out teletype reports. We sent coded readings of our own observations and received them from hundreds of other stations. The forecasters analyzed the maps, made their best guesses and briefed the pilot-training groups at Roswell. The base there was a good-sized installation then.

Q: And years later you returned to Roswell to work, didn't you?

A: In 1959–1960, I taught English at the New Mexico Military Institute. I lived on the campus but for the life of me I can't remember anyone speaking of the UFO incident. I don't recall the first time I heard of the incident.

Q: What do you make of the good, solid citizens of Roswell who have stuck to their stories about the incident for years and years? I'm thinking of, say, Glenn Dennis, the undertaker who has always maintained that in July 1947 he received a telephone call from the base inquiring about child-sized coffins and embalming procedures and that he knew a nurse at the base who told him she witnessed the alien autopsy.

A: Memories are incredible things. You have these accounts of how memories are changed and not changed.

Q: Has your training as a scientist helped you as a writer?

A: I set out to major in chemistry, at West Texas State College. Then I studied psychology and physics. I studied astronomy for a while at Berkeley. I stay up with the science field. I subscribe to *Science, Science News, Scientific American, Astronomy*, computer magazines. Most science-fiction writers know a good deal of science. Enough to examine evidence of UFOs and to know that it's not there or it's badly flawed. UFO people generally are not scientifically trained.

Q: The first unidentified flying object in New Mexico was reported near Lamy, in the late 1800s. It was a balloon in the shape of a fish, a newspaper article said, and it had eight or ten persons in it. Some kind of party, it sounds like to me. I know you didn't see that particular UFO, but have you ever seen one?

A: [*Laughs.*] No, though I know various people who have reported them. But I don't think they saw something. What they may have seen was bright planets or lenticular clouds that played tricks on their eyes.

Q: How close do you think you've come to seeing a UFO?

A: Fred Pohl, a writer friend who has collaborated with me on many projects, and like me was sort of a skeptic but was interested in people and how they act. In 1964, after that one UFO was reportedly seen in Socorro, New Mexico, by the city policeman there, a famous case, Fred and I went down there soon after it happened. The site had been marked by rocks. You could see depressions of landing gear on the ground. Grass had been burned by the craft's jets, so evidence was still fresh. But the prints formed an imperfect rectangle, the impressions displaced as if to avoid rocks in the way of a square-pointed shovel. The brush was burned close to the ground where there had been dry grass, but not at the top, where a hot jet might ignite it.

Q: What did all this mean to you?

A: I immediately thought, and still do think, that students from Socorro, from the New Mexico School of Mines, only a mile or so away, did it. Played a hoax. I've known lots of students and I've seen what an enterprising student can do. I'm convinced the students had arranged for the cop to be watching while they sent up a balloon equipped with lights and noisemakers. I think that policeman was an honest cop and saw something take off, just south of town, but he didn't see the real thing.

Q: Some debunkers think the Socorro incident—the little men in white coveralls standing by an egg-shaped object on stilts—was staged by town officials who hoped to bring in more tourists to a community that seemed starved for industry. Any reaction?

A: That sounds more like what has happened in Roswell. I still think the kids in Socorro did it. I don't think Chamber of Commerce officials there would be so clever.

Q: The recent movie *Contact*, made from Carl Sagan's novel about a search for the extraterrestrial, featured an elaborate hoax. Why is the UFO terrain so littered with hoaxes?

A: Let's just say there are people in the field who are frauds. I don't want to say names. I believe there are people who will invent stories. The country today has a great surplus of paranoia. I don't think any one person can control it. But it has snowballed, like an urban myth.

Q: Though many Americans would like to think of themselves as Christians, there are more alien abductions reported each year than sightings of Jesus or the Virgin Mary. Any thoughts?

A: Alien abductions remind me of stories about therapists who get other people to discover memories of childhood abuse. I think a good therapist can make a person believe he's been abducted. An alien abduction is hard for people to accept—and it should be.

Q: You could live anywhere you want. Why Portales?

A: People are friendly here, they treat me well, it's a wonderful place. I came to this county first, as a young boy, in 1915, in a covered wagon. My Dad homesteaded here. I was born in Arizona Territory, but then we got a hardscrabble farm on a place thirty-five miles from Portales, a little place called Richland, New Mexico. I went to Richland High School. It wasn't even accredited. It's gone now and so is Richland, for the most part. But Portales is still about the same size—10,000 people and 4,000 more at the university. The name, incidentally, comes from springs that resembled a porch on a Spanish ranch house.

Q: Were you a reader as a child?

A: Oh, yes. Dad had gone to college and so books weren't unusual, even in this rural setting. I read Jules Verne, H.G. Wells, Edgar Rice Burroughs.

Q: When did you start writing science fiction?

A: In 1928, when I was a college student, in Canyon, Texas, I sent Hugo Gernsback, editor of the recently launched *Amazing Stories*, the first science-fiction magazine, a story I had written. I called it "The Metal Man." I wrote it on an old Remington, which

129

I used for years. I had sent Gernsback stories before but this one never came back. Then one day I was walking past a drugstore in Canyon and saw the words "The Metal Man" featured on the outside cover of a magazine. I recognized them as my title, my story. It was a great moment for me.

Q: The whole field of science-fiction was so very young then, wasn't it?

A: It was called *scientifiction* in those days, a term invented by Gernsback. In 1929, he changed it to *science fiction*. Early on it was hard to sell science-fiction to publishers. Science-fiction was a pretty lonely and neglected enterprise for many years. There were just pulp magazines for years, which I contributed to. When I finally got a book published, in 1947, it was a big event.

Q: Eventually you went on to teach English?

A: Yes, I received my doctorate from Colorado, at a late age, at fifty-six. I wanted to be around students. But I wanted to be around science-fiction, too. I wrote my dissertation on H.G. Wells, about his early science-fiction. He pioneered most of the major themes in the field. He was an important person in my life.

Q: Despite science-fiction's great growth, some people still don't accept it. Why?

A: I've encountered people all my life who have thought science-fiction was fluff, that it was sub-literate nonsense. They have a right to their opinion.

Q: The eminent fantasy writer Theodore Sturgeon called ninety percent of science-fiction crap. But then he added that ninety percent of *everything* was crap. Your feelings?

A: There is a lot of material being published, yes. Last I heard almost 3,000 new science-fiction titles a year. Staggering. Some good, some not so good, I'm sorry to say. But that happens whenever there is a surge in production of any product.

Q: You've been a prime mover in establishing science fiction as a respectable academic discipline. And you've been a part of it all—from the pulpy to the literate. Science fiction has come a long way, hasn't it?

A: When I was writing science fiction in the 1930s, I never made more than $1,452 in a single year. As an academic discipline, science fiction offers an obvious parallel. I've always been interested in the frontier life, starting when I was a boy when I read the writings of Walter Prescott Webb, who saw modern history as being shaped by what he called the Great Frontier. In science fiction, we're always dealing with the frontiers of space, of knowledge, of astronomy, biology, and nuclear physics.

Q: Then science fiction looks at the future?

A: Science fiction looks at possibilities. Basically, it explores the ideas that have impacted technology. It tells what *might* happen in the future. It doesn't predict, but it examines possible futures. Science fiction claims credit sometimes for anticipating things that really happened. But it's a shotgun approach. If you forecast everything, you're bound to hit some things. And in different countries, there's a whole new psychology. In Africa and India, science fiction is almost unknown.

Q: So what's *sci-fi*?

A: Sci-fi is the shortened form for people too lazy. A bastardization. That's where popular culture has really led us, I'm afraid: to the shortened form of life.

Q: What are you working on now?

A: I still enjoy writing novels, and I hope to have one published next year. I work every day on it. At my age, I don't have a great deal of energy. But I work four hours a day in four different shifts.

Q: You appear to be in good health.
A: Oh, I have an aching back from hunching over a computer. You know, I bought my first computer in 1979.

Q: Why haven't any of your books been made into movies?
A: Several have been optioned. People occasionally rewrite a script. I sold my first story to the movies fifty years ago. To American International. It was never produced. It would be nice to have a piece of that money. But I don't know what I'd spend it on now.

chapter 7

Making Movies by the Numbers

"Like Hollywood, Roswell is in the fantasy business."
— *Forbes*, 1996

ALMOST EVERY SCIENCE-FICTION MOVIE that dealt with aliens, from the 1950s until decades later, followed a set of regulations that should be called the Roswell Rules. These standards take their properties directly from what's been reported about New Mexico's prominent UFO incident. In movies that observe the Roswell Rules, the following situations always apply:

Radar screens and towers must be introduced early on.

All technicians must wear white lab coats or decontamination suits.

The military must be involved and must be trigger-happy.

There must be a moral.

Two films that use the Roswell Rules to greatest affect, that seem almost by the numbers guardians of those edicts, are *The Day the Earth Stood Still* and *Invaders From Mars*. Both movies are hallmarks in terms of science-fiction celluloid. More important, each was directly impacted by happenings that emanated from southeast New Mexico. Indeed, looking at those movies today one has to believe that the movies' makers knew a substantial amount about the classified events of July 1947 and utilized many of those reports to spin out their stories.

Before there were science-fiction movies of any kind, however, there was radio, and to fully understand the principles of the Roswell Rules, one must first consider a celebrated occurrence in that medium. Nearly ten years before there was a Roswell, New Mexico, incident, there was a Grover's Mill, New Jersey, incident. Grover's Mill, of course, was the site of a Martian landing in Orson Welles's famed modernized radio version of H.G. Wells's novel *The War of the Worlds*.

Broadcast nationwide on Halloween Eve, 1938, with only periodic disclaimers, the radio show caused an immediate uproar. Thousands of people, believing that Martian poison gas was spreading death and destruction over the East Coast, began to leave their houses to speed to what they thought might be safety. Others armed themselves to fight the invaders.

Welles initially denied that he wanted to cause trouble; his only purpose in doing the drama, he said, was to entertain. Still, he admitted he yearned to take a slap at radio—for having too much authority. UFO conspiracy followers believe that the United States government took it as a lesson to be used later. When something momentous happens, the lesson went, don't let it get any bigger than you have to, or civilians will act as they did in 1938: they will panic.

Indeed, that's what an Associated Press front-page story in the *Roswell Daily Record* of October 31, 1938 was headlined. "RADIO BRINGS PANIC TO MANY IN THE NATION."

No one living in Roswell in 1938 remembers great pandemonium there, though Frank Joyce, then a local youth of fifteen, recollects running outside his house that evening and carrying a rifle. Roswell's lone radio station had as usual signed off at 7:00 P.M.

134

that Sunday night, so Joyce and others, as they frequently did, tuned in a power station, such as one out of Fort Worth, Texas, or perhaps Shreveport, Louisiana. "A neighbor man saw me hurry out into the street that night with a shotgun," Joyce recalls laughing, "and he said, 'Whaddya doin'?' I said, 'Well, the Martians are comin'.'"

If Orson Welles offered nourishment to the idea that aliens could roam New Jersey, the far-and-wide UFO sightings of 1947 offered vigor to the idea that aliens could be found nationwide. In truth, aliens *everywhere* had been a concept for a while. During the war, allied fliers over Germany had reported strange glowing disks and lights and called them "foo fighters," from a maxim by a cartoon character named Smokey Stover, who was fond of saying, "Where there's foo, there's fire." (In an odd turn of events that may justify the logic of the Coincidental Corollary, the Foo Fighters, a rock 'n' roll band, provided some of the music for the 1998 movie *The X-Files*). Kenneth Arnold gave those disks the real boost, however. Arnold, from Boise, Idaho, sold fire extinguishers so well that he owned his own aircraft. On June 24, 1947, piloting his small plane in Washington state during a business trip, Arnold spotted near him in the air nine silver objects that zipped by like a flock of geese. The disks seemed to resemble boomerangs, or maybe saucers skipping over the water, Arnold told reporters, who quickly dubbed them "flying saucers." During the next few weeks, flying saucers were seen coming out of the clouds in nearly ever state. Arnold went on to observe several more sightings before his death in 1984.

Through the years, UFO partisans have argued that Kenneth Arnold's disclosure and the Roswell incident were dismissed by the government in order to quell a *War of the Worlds* panic. Such arguments only served to plant more ideas in more people that saucers were real. After all, the arguers maintained, the Air Force had noted 122 flying-saucer sightings in 1947, the first year such records were kept. Twelve sightings that year went unidentified and one UFO researcher says 850 more reports weren't even recorded during the twelve months.

With the foundation poured by Welles, the events of '47, and a renewed interest in science fiction, Hollywood grew interested. Movie studios quickly filled an entertainment void with this theme: creatures from outer space can drop in on us any time they wish. Americans were coaxed by the media into accepting that theme, or at least acknowledging that it might have validity. When radio personality Arthur Godfrey, who enjoyed a huge following, perhaps the largest fan base in the country, announced in 1950 that he had been buzzed by a flying saucer while piloting his plane, the gears started turning in earnest. Popular uproar grew with each year; and along with radioactivity and communism flying saucers touched a raw nerve with the public. *Destination Moon*, which opened in 1950, set off a torrent of science-fiction films in the fifties.

But it was *The Thing From Another World*, released in 1951, that laid the groundwork for the Roswell Rules. In that film, a pie-plate saucer crashes in the North Pole with an alien lifeform aboard. A snoopy journalist causes the government to fear that if word got out about the event, people would take fright. Later that year came *The Day the Earth Stood Still*. The movie takes what had possibly occurred in the New Mexico desert in 1947 and adds a strange twist to the position of UFOs in popular culture. Instead of being solely based on incidents, the movie may have sparked an incident. On July 19, 1952, a year after *The Day the Earth Stood Still* opened in theaters across the country, seven slow moving objects showed up on radar at National Airport and Andrews Air Force Base. A week later, another set of objects appeared again over Washington, D.C. One headline read:

FIERY OBJECTS OUTRUN JETS OVER CAPITAL
INVESTIGATION VEILED IN SECRECY
FOLLOWING VAIN CHASE

136

Filmed in black and white, and directed by Robert Wise, *The Day the Earth Stood Still* set a high standard for films that followed—particularly science-fiction films. Edmund North wrote the screenplay and based it on a Harry Bates short story, "Farewell to the Master," that originally appeared in *Astounding* magazine. The big difference between *The Day the Earth Stood Still* and other flying saucer movies is that Klaatu, the alien aboard the craft that touches down in Washington, D.C., comes seeking peace, not destruction. Klaatu, a humanoid, is draped in gray, the color witnesses have most frequently used to describe the Roswell aliens. The difference is that this alien speaks. Klaatu is disturbed, he says, by the troubled times on Earth, particularly the postwar paranoia over communism. Klaatu wants to get the world leaders together to discuss peace and goodwill before the planet blows itself to smithereens. If Klaatu senses something on the horizon, he is prescient: on November 1, 1952, the United States tested its first thermonuclear device, on Enwietok, in the Pacific, generating a force 1,000 times greater than Hiroshima. The Russians completed their first nuclear test on August 12, 1953.

Even though they are backed by tanks and artillery, Army troopers suddenly panic, shoot and wound Klaatu. (Popular culture is derivative: Coast Guardsmen or Marines rarely confront aliens; it's almost always soldiers, as if taking a lead from Roswell, where the Army Air Force reportedly reached the crash site early, in order to clean things up and, according to UFO researchers, to erase the entire event from history, to "neutralize" it, as depicted in the movie *Men in Black*, 1997.)

Taken to Walter Reed Hospital—in the same manner that aliens in Roswell were supposedly transported to that city's Army Air Force hospital and then autopsied—Klaatu later escapes from a ward. Now disguised as an Earthling, he moves about Washington, where he makes friends with a woman and her young son, and tries to spread his olive-branch gospel. Even when Klaatu proves his point that people of the world must listen to him—he halts all traffic, stops clothes dryers, and turns off outboard motors—few want to really believe him. He's jailed and eventually freed by his chilling Frankenstein-monster-like robot Gort. The two go back to their parked saucer in the Capitol mall, Klaatu delivers one final warning, guns his spaceship and is gone.

From the film's opening shot of spinning radar towers, a viewer knows *The Day the Earth Stood Still* is obeying the Roswell Rules. Several accounts have said that at least three radar stations in southern New Mexico had been tracking an unidentified flying object in the skies since July 1, 1947. The object had allegedly been first detected over White Sands Proving Grounds, where secret missile tests were conducted. During the evening of July 4, supposedly an unidentified radar target brightened and faded, then brightened again to a "sunburst" and disappeared entirely at 11:20 P.M.

The Roswell object was considered to move at "incredible speeds," says writer Kevin D. Randle. The spacecraft in *The Day the Earth Stood Still* travels at 4,000 miles per hour. Confronted with the saucer in *The Day the Earth Stood Still,* the Army tries and fails to blowtorch the shell of the vessel. In 1947, Major Jesse Marcel Sr., the Roswell base's intelligence officer, found he couldn't burn the recovered debris with a cigarette lighter. Klaatu worries about warfare testing done in America, and in 1947 New Mexico had the only atomic bomb. Finally, that Gort is a robot makes complete sense in light that several accounts from Roswell speculated that the aliens that came in 1947 were robotic in nature, automatons guided by an outside force.

All by himself, then, Gort launched a batch of robot movies, from *Robot Monster* (1953) to *The Robot vs. the Aztec Mummy* (1959). Most are awful and yet all share this pedigree: they have something to do with Roswell.

Contrary to widespread belief, *The Day the Earth Stood Still* was not the first UFO movie. *Flying Saucer*, a minor effort produced independently in 1949 and never released nationally, gets that honor. A government agent investigating strange sightings uncovers in

Flying Saucer a double horror: an alien craft and Russians up to no good. Four years after the Washington D.C. sightings made headlines, the nation's capital became the scene of another motion picture scare, *Earth vs. the Flying Saucers*, in which a bevy of disk-shaped saucers attack the District of Columbia.

The Day the Earth Stood Still's saucer first appears on screen as a prototypical Mexican sombrero, humming like a blender. Its size is what stuns the audience. Silver in color, the saucer measures 350 feet in diameter and stands 25 feet high. It was said to cost M-G-M $100,000, an immense sum at the time.

Gort, Klaatu's traveling companion in the spaceship, was not filmdom's first walking bucket of bolts. One must go back to Golem, a female robot in Fritz Lang's 1926 creation, *Metropolis*. However, Gort, so clunking and yet so foreboding, was the most indestructible robot of his time. Curiously, in the original short story, the robot was the master and Klaatu acted as his servant. In the film, Gort, played by seven-foot-tall actor Lock Martin, never appears in a scene in which he doesn't cause immediate terror.

The Day the Earth Stood Still, like Orson Welles's radio broadcast of 1938, seems credible. Drew Pearson, the celebrated radio and TV broadcaster of the era, wears a snap-brim hat in the studio when he delivers the news flashes in his familiar clipped style. "The arrival of a spaceship is no cause for alarm . . . it landed at 3:47 P.M. . . . we don't know where it came from." News personalities H.V. Kaltenborn and Gabriel Heater also are on hand to present bulletins about the landing. The appearance of those three adds a special touch of realism to the movie, just as if Tom Brokaw, Peter Jennings and Dan Rather would if they had turned up holding microphones in *Independence Day*.

As *The War of the Worlds* radio broadcast did, *The Day the Earth Stood Still* accentuates a fear of the unknown. The United States at the time was experiencing A-bomb anxiety. To substantiate that uneasiness, the film aligned those feelings with an alien invasion. Indeed, Klaatu announces: "We know your planet has discovered a rudimentary form of atomic energy and that you're experimenting with rockets . . . soon, one of your nations will apply atomic energy to spaceships and that will create a threat to the peace and security of other planets. That, of course, we cannot tolerate."

Christian symbolism is woven through *The Day the Earth Stood Still*, and the movie was readily accepted in Roswell, where the sound of churchbells has always filled the air on Sunday morning. Klaatu, as portrayed by the serene British actor Michael Rennie, takes the disguise of Major "Carpenter" to offer mankind salvation from holocaust. In the movie, Carpenter is betrayed and then imprisoned by soldiers. When Gort melts a wall of the jail to free his master, it's as if someone is rolling away a stone from Jesus's tomb. When Klaatu finally departs Earth, it's his Ascension that appears to be the last chance for man.

So a conversion begins. We're helped in our new beliefs by having empathy for the people Klaatu touches—Helen (Patrica Neal) and her young son Bobby (Billy Gray). Both of those characters think of the space alien as a person and not a thing, a rare event in science-fiction films—then or now. Even if we're agnostic, we have reasons to look up to Klaatu. In the way he changes his clothes—from alien to Carpenter to alien again—he's like another hero of popular culture, Superman.

Even the humming noise of the saucer plays a role in our conversion, and it's no wonder. Bernard Hermann, the composer who created the music for Orson Welles's Mercury Theater version of *The War of the Worlds,* created the eerie electronic score for *The Day the Earth Stood Still.*

As serious as the message is in *The Day the Earth Stood Still*, the movie offers sly humor, which also helps to explain the film's success. A woman who doesn't know that Rennie/Carpenter is the alien, says to him, as one might say to a stranger:

"You're a long way from home, aren't you?"

When someone mentions spacemen invading, a skeptic rolls his eyes and says, as one would say of a deranged person:

"They wouldn't come in spaceships; they'd come in airplanes." When Klaatu is asked how much he knows of astrophysics, he answers as one might when confronted with a silly question: "Well enough to get me from one planet to another."

Despite its adherence to the Roswell Rules, *The Day the Earth Stood Still* has moments of incredulity. As the saucer and robot sit in wait on the mall in Washington, D.C., only two soldiers are assigned to stand guard. (At least two dozen armed troopers were said to flank the Roswell ship.) Yet it's the message of the movie—that global peace is still an elusive goal—that holds up almost fifty years later. During a visit to Arlington National Cemetery, when Klaatu tells young Bobby that his planet has no wars, we know that something is wrong in our world. And of course there is the message bound in Klaatu's final reminder:

"I came here to warn you that by threatening danger, your planet faces grave danger."

The Day the Earth Stood Still not only served as a standard-bearer for other science-fiction movies of the decade, but it gave Klaatu an enduring fame. For generations of moviegoers, Patricia Neal's peculiar line to Gort, asking for help to rescue his master, became a celebrated chant: "*Klaatu borada nikto.*" In the 1970s, a rock music group named itself *Klaatu*. Ringo Starr further enshrined Klaatu by putting the alien, Gort, and himself on the rim of a flying saucer and making that the cover of his album "Goodnight Vienna."

Even renowned anthropologist Margaret Mead must have been a fan of *The Day the Earth Stood Still*. In a 1974 article in *Redbook* magazine, Mead writes of UFOs: "the most likely explanation, it seems to me, is that they (aliens) are simply watching what we are up to—that a responsible society outside our solar system is keeping an eye on us to see that we don't set in motion a chain reaction that might have repercussions far outside our solar system."

The movie's status in the pantheon of popular culture was solidified when the first major catalog of feature film cassettes for home videotape players was released in 1978. *The Day the Earth*

Stood Still was the single science-fiction offering from the 1950s, a decade that produced thousands of reels of sci-fi footage.

Thirty years after *The Day the Earth Stood Still* appeared, the idea that a space alien could come to Earth as a gentle soul still mesmerized Hollywood. *Starman*, released in 1984, starred Jeff Bridges as an alien who crashlands his spaceship in rural Wisconsin. (The Coincidental Corollary can be seen again: during the early 1950s the Aerial Phenomena Research Organization, which tracked all information on flying saucers, was located in rural Wisconsin. Later, it moved to New Mexico, to Holloman Air Force Base at Alamogordo.) Bridges takes the form of a human and becomes a figure of great benevolence: he restores life to a dead deer, and he impregnates a woman who never thought she could conceive.

"What's it like up there?" Starman is asked.

Klaatu-like, Bridges answers, "No war . . . no hunger . . . the strong do not victimize the helpless . . . we are very civilized."

The Man Who Fell to Earth (1976) features a similarly calm visitor from outer space. Fragile, pale Thomas Newton, a defier of gravity played by rocker David Bowie, has come to Earth to seek water. Newton's planet is suffering from a severe drought, and he is desperate for a means of bringing liquid to his wife and two children, who are dying of dehydration. Filmed partly in Artesia, thirty miles south of Roswell, *The Man Who Fell to Earth* offers some of the same shrewd double-entendres as *The Day the Earth Stood Still*.

Girl: "What do you do for a living?"

Bowie: "Just visiting. . . ."

Girl: "Oh, a traveler."

Later, the same girl, a motel maid in Artesia, a city that might as well be Roswell, says words that any UFO investigator can appreciate: "What do you want to go back to a desert for? We got deserts here."

If *The Man Who Fell to Earth* reminds us of anything, it's that fantasy can sometimes be confused with reality. Apollo 13 astronaut James Lovell, who almost fell out of the stratosphere himself in 1970, plays a cameo role in the movie.

The year 1953 was a vintage one for science-fiction films and releases ranged from *Them!* to *Donovan's Brain* to *The Beast From 20,000 Fathoms.* To some degree, all paid attention to the Roswell Rules, particularly lab personnel in white smocks who stare wide-eyed at radar screens, and Army troops who shoot first and ask questions later. *The War of the Worlds,* which also rolled across the screen that year, tooks things a step further. The film actually mentions, if obliquely, the 1947 incident in New Mexico. When an airplane flown by Dr. Clayton Forrester (Gene Barry), an astro-physicist, is shot down by Martians, it crashes in a barren patch of what appears to be the Southwest, clearly a clever reversal of the Desert Dictum. Forrester's female companion (Ann Robinson) asks Forrester where they are.

"Southwest of Corona," says Forrester, mentioning the nearest New Mexico village to the debris field stumbled upon by Mack Brazel in 1947 "There must have been another cylinder down here. They've been through this whole area and cleaned everybody out."

Forrester's character is based loosely on Dr. Lincoln LaPaz, a dashing, square-jawed mathematician who founded the University of New Mexico Institute of Meteoritics in 1944 and remained its director until 1966. LaPaz had studied incendiary bombs carried by Japanese paper balloons during World War II, and he had examined the Socorro incident in 1964, which he blamed on a vertical short takeoff and landing aircraft, used by the military. In 1947, the government had summoned LaPaz, who held a top-secret clearance, to Roswell to inspect the debris field. LaPaz's findings never were made public, but a few years later he told a reporter, "There is no need to believe we are being invaded from outer space. Anyone living outside this troubled globe would be displaying absolute nonsense to come here."

In terms of impacting the popular culture of UFOs, no 1953 science-fiction movie can come close to *Invaders From Mars.* Upon its release, *Invaders From Mars* did not enjoy the same applause heaped on *The Day the Earth Stood Still*. Indeed, some critics who loved *The Day* dismissed *Invaders* as bunkum. "Funnybook . . . full of impossible action and childish imaginings," said *The New York Times*. Despite such ridicule, *Invaders From Mars* today is considered an astonishing accomplishment. Directed by the esteemed William Cameron Menzies who, in 1934, had designed and put together the movie *Things to Come* from the H.G. Wells's novel, *Invaders From Mars* was a success at the box office. More important to its makers, *Invaders* beat out by six months the release of *The War of the Worlds*.

Invaders, just as much as *The Day the Earth Stood Still*, built upon the growing, xenophobic, Roswell-reinforced angst of the times. And, maybe more than *The Day*, *Invaders* has since become a cult classic. Though it appears to have been turned out swiftly and cheaply, *Invaders* stands out, particularly for its use of color and lighting.

As with many science-fiction films of the fifties, *Invaders From Mars* draws from the pulp fiction conventions that had dominated science fiction since the 1920s. Invasions from space, stalwart heroes, beautiful heroines, heat rays, and bug-eyed aliens were all part of science fiction's stock-in-trade during the genre's adolescence.

It's true that *Invaders* kept things simple, that it was and is pure escapism—on one level. Earthmen versus aliens, good versus evil, us versus them. But there are many levels to this picture. David MacLean, (Jimmy Hunt), is the hero of *Invaders*. Like *The Day the Earth Stood Still*'s Bobby Benson, an innocent, wonder-struck boy is this movie's chief protagonist. David rescues Army troops in an underground grotto with a motion ray gun only he can operate. Only David can spot the differences between normal people and those enslaved by the Martians. Only David can alert others that something is very wrong.

The figure of the child is significant in science fiction of the fifties, and director Steven Spielberg drew on that knowledge years later when he created his two masterpieces, *Close Encounters of the Third Kind* and *E.T., The Extraterrestrial (1982)*. In *Close Encounters*, four-year-old Barry Guiler (Cary Guffey) is kidnapped by a UFO. In *E.T.*, ten-year-old Elliott (Henry Thomas) is the befriender of a Reece's Pieces-loving alien. While each child is intrepid, neither is like the boy-heroes of *The Day the Earth Stood Still* and *Invaders From Mars*, which turn their children into John Waynes. The young boys of these two movies represent a version of ourselves: Bobby and David are what we hoped we could be. They can believe anything and do anything and look upon tomorrow as a time when anything can happen. It's a belief that Jesse Marcel Jr. epitomized in the Roswell incident. When his father one night brought home to show young Jesse pieces of what the senior Marcel believed were outer space debris, little Jesse, wearing pajamas, looked on with eyes the size of oysters.

Both *The Day the Earth Stood Still* and *Invaders From Mars* involve child-parent relationships, as did the Roswell incident. On July 5, 1947, when ranch foreman Mack Brazel went out near Corona, New Mexico, to inspect the pastures of what later became known as the debris field, a large stretch of sinkholes, depressions, and sagebrush, he brought with him William "Dee" Proctor, a neighbor boy, about the same age as Bobby Benson and David MacLean. Brazel and young Proctor found scattered all across the slopes of the Foster ranchland northwest of Roswell, metal and plastic-like beams, lightweight sticks, pieces of sturdy string and tinfoil. There's so much junk strewn about the field that sheep refuse to cross the plain and have to be led to a waterhole a mile away.

Believing at first their discovery might be a giant kite, Brazel and Dee Proctor actually spend several minutes attempting to *fly* the debris. Curiously, Elliott, whose father in *E.T.* is divorced from his mother, goes alone to a clearing in a forest and single-handedly helps his alien friend rig up a transmitter that uses debris, including a circular saw, umbrella, and tinfoil.

Debris and the work it entails to remove it, have intrigued movie-makers since the Roswell incident. For reasons of its own, Hollywood found a strong bond between space travel and janitors. Roswell likely influenced this thinking, for one luminary there, according to some UFO chronologists, was Warrant Officer Robert Thomas, in charge of the clean-up at the alleged site the day after. Indeed, Thomas and his team reportedly swept spotless the ground where the spacecraft supposedly fell. They did such a good job that they erased for everyone any physical sign that the incident happened. And yet at the same time that fine job by these picker-uppers caused countless people to believe it *did* happen.

This trend, call it the Cosmos Custodian Doctrine, began in theaters in 1953 with *Abbott and Costello Go to Mars*. The janitorial pair is tidying up around a rocket ship one day when suddenly they're lifting off to the Red Planet. (To ask how that ever happened is to ask why aliens don't wear toreador pants or dinner jackets.) Anyway, Abbott and Costello's rocket eventually lands not on Mars, but on Venus, which is populated by bathing beauties. (Again, don't ask.) The Cosmos Custodian Doctrine reappears in *The Three Stooges in Orbit* (1962), in which the broom-pushing Stooges, also due to reasons too complicated to explain, find themselves headed for Mars. Their craft is a propeller-driven tugboat but one should fear not; the Stooges are space experts, as they so adeptly proved in *Have Rocket Will Travel* (1959). Don Knotts spends his days moving a mop at NASA headquarters in Houston until someone in *The Reluctant Astronaut* (1967) decides that Knotts should be steering a space capsule, beating the Russians to Mars. The truth is up there: on the big screen, Knotts bore great facial resemblance to astronaut Alan Shepard.

O.J. Simpson had no floors to polish in *Capricorn One* (1978), but as an astronaut on a phony voyage to Mars Simpson had to huff and puff to make us believe he really was one of NASA's finest. (His first line in the movie: "I think I'm gonna throw up.") Of interest to Roswell anthropologists: the fraudulent journey in *Capri-*

corn One takes place in a hangar on an Army Air Base set in Texas—"abandoned," indicates a sign in the film, "in 1947."

A warm-hearted scientist rather than a dustpan-holding laborer takes an important role in both *The Day the Earth Stood Still* and *Invaders From Mars*. In *The Day the Earth Stood Still*, it's Albert Einstein-like Professor Barnhart. In *Invaders From Mars*, it's Dr. Stuart Kelston, a *Mr. Wizard* sort of astronomer: "Here, David, let me show you how to use this retractable lens. . . ."

The message is clear: events such as Roswell drew scientists, but most of those men were cold and unfriendly and likely worked for the government. Surely if those scientists had only been like Professor Barnhart and Dr. Kelston, well, we would be so much better off.

Finally, *The Day* and *Invaders* offer as a central character an adult woman who is sympathetic to the young boy in the story and so attractive to the aliens that they wind up carrying her in their arms. The counterpart in the Roswell incident would be Loretta Proctor, young Dee's mother, said to be enchantingly downhome.

The flying saucer of *Invaders From Mars* is hardly as fearsome looking as the one in *The Day the Earth Stood Still*. Nevertheless, it chills us. We see it early, as we do the one in *The Day the Earth Stood Still*, just as young David spots it from his bedroom window. The craft plunks down in Coral Bluffs, the sandhills behind David's house, and the geographic reference is obvious: Coral Bluffs is the White Sands Proving Grounds, which in 1947 was said to be a likely magnet for curious alien visitors. Adjoining Coral Bluffs stands the Armstead plant, where David's father works and which is rumored to be making all sorts of top secret rockets, just like postwar White Sands, or the Roswell Army Air Field which in 1947 harbored an atomic bomb.

Invaders From Mars originally was meant to be the first science-fiction 3-D movie, but that idea eventually was scrapped. Even in two dimensions it's a muddled story, however. A young boy who witnesses a Martian landing soon recognizes the way the invaders take over the brains of Earth dwellers by implanting crystals in the backs of necks of anyone who falls into the sand pit behind the MacLean house. Accompanied by "The Cassions Go Rolling Along," the Army arrives as usual, with all kinds of heavy firepower. "If it's a fight they want, they're gonna get it," says Colonel Fielding, played by Morris Ankrum, a journeyman actor who defined the role of the impetuous and stubborn military officer. His equal in Roswell? Colonel William H. "Butch" Blanchard, commander of the 509th Heavy Bomber Wing at Roswell Army Air Field in 1947. Blanchard had ordered the famous "Flying Disk Recovered" press release and the following day had changed the story to read a weather balloon, on orders from his superior officer in Texas. On May 31, 1966, the hard-charging Blanchard suffered a heart attack at a desk in the Pentagon. A decorated B-29 pilot in the war, Blanchard was the second-ranking officer in the Air Force when he died, at age fifty. Ankrum built a career out of parts in science-fiction movies of the fifties. In addition to *Invaders From Mars*, Ankrum's credits include: *Rocketship to the Moon* (1950); *Flight to Mars* (1951); *Red Planet Mars* (1952); *Earth vs. the Flying Saucers* (1956); *From the Earth to the Moon* (1958).

The arrival of Colonel Fielding and his troops brings about an underground battle, with young David leading the way against aliens, all large and as ugly as mud fences. One of the aliens is played by the same Lock Martin who, coincidentally, wore Gort's robot armament in *The Day the Earth Stood Still*.

Invaders From Mars engenders the same kind of flying-saucer hysteria as seen in *The Day the Earth Stood Still*. The Martians who want to get their green mitts on that rocket ship at the Armstead plant and use it to get back to their planet, turn the Earthlings into walking zombies to help them. David's father George MacLean (Leif Erickson) suffers from so much mind-control—like others afflicted, a red hole has been drilled in the base of his brain by the Invaders—that he smacks his son. You know the abuse is far out of character, but it's so frightening that you don't know what can be done about it.

Like *The Day the Earth Stood Still*, *Invaders* possesses strong religious elements. In a series of placidly beautiful scenes, young David watches as victim after victim falls into the Martian sandtrap, as if being won over to a new and tranquil faith. Meanwhile, a Hallelujah chorus provides background music. It took thirty years of horrifying space monsters before this charitable, quasi-spiritual attitude could be seen again, specifically in the goodness of the aliens found in *Close Encounters* and *E.T.*

When young David finally goes to the police station to ask for help for his parents and others similarly brainwashed, the resulting scene is downright scary. The station is bare and white and David's smallness in that stark emptiness is intensified. (It's surely a similar feeling that small-in-stature Mack Brazel must have experienced when the Roswell base security squad detained him for nearly a week in 1947.) In fact, the camera takes the same angle to shoot David talking to an adult as it did when *The Day's* Bobby Benson had a heart-to-heart talk with Klaatu.

A hefty dose of sexuality permeates *Invaders From Mars*. David is helped by a pretty young nurse (actress Helena Carter, in her final movie) and as she takes the part of his mother, she nearly receives one of those awful neck implants. Though no record exists of anyone being implanted at Roswell, a pretty young nurse does figure in accounts of the incident. Mortuary worker Glenn Dennis said the woman, who worked at the Roswell Army Air Field hospital, relayed to him in July 1947 the terrifying information that an autopsy on space creatures had just been performed at the base.

While Klaatu bears goodwill, the hideous mutants in *Invaders From Mars* have no such generosity on their minds. Covered by a green woolly skin, their heads a lollipop of knobs, the invaders hold in their hands what appear to be jumbo-sized toilet plungers. "Big apes," the soldiers call the creatures. They lumber around below ground, controlled by their master, a ghastly looking head that rests inside a fishbowl and that silently gives commands by darting its eyes back and forth.

There is silliness in *Invaders*, as there was in *The Day the Earth Stood Still*. Dr. Wilson, the prominent physicist at the Armstead rocket plant, is shown handling test tubes, as a chemist might. The Army has stopped the mutants' brain-control device with this easily understandable solution: "We've rigged the original crystal to a variable oscillator." When the mutants' saucer explodes at the end of the movie in a stirring detonation, only one small tree falls over.

In defense of some of the film's awkwardness, Menzies's original storyboards became lost during shooting and much improvising had to be done, particularly toward the end. That explains why the Martians are seen loping aimlessly about the grotto, back and forth. It was simply an attempt to add minutes to the movie.

Invaders brings to the screen no great revelations about science. In fact, it took a slap at science fiction—when David's mother berates him for reading trashy sci-fi magazines. Instead, *Invaders* offers powerful visual images and in doing so reflects the secret hopes and desires in all of us. If the movie speaks any language, it's the language of dreams and nightmares.

Invaders shows that Good Guys can win. "We'll blow them all the way back to Mars," promises Colonel Fielding. Young David helps to rescue alluring Helena Carter before a crystal is rammed into the base of her brain. Moreover, the grotto is an interesting place. Menzies's design for the odd-shaped bunching on the tunnel walls was implemented by using ordinary rubber prophylactics.

Not long after the Martian ship detonates, David wakes up in his bedroom. Was he having a dream? Hard to say. In fact, the movie developed two endings. The original conclusion was reshot for European audiences. David looks out the window and once again sees another spaceship coming to land. The story starts all over again, sort of a *Groundhog Day* (1993) with the willies. In another ending, David wakes up and tells his dad he was having a bad dream, about aliens. "They were green," he says, "and had a ray gun."

Go to sleep, David's father urges, though that's not so easy to do after watching this film.

Invaders From Mars bred a legion of imitators, most of them dreadful. A few of the copycats: *Flight to Mars* (1952), *They Came From Beyond Space* (1967), and *Don't Play With Martians* (1967). In 1959, a New Jersey man named Howard Menger, who had claimed to be a contactee and had made frequent appearances on Long John Nebel's celebrated WOR radio show in New York City, published *From Outer Space to You*. In the book, Menger talked about his various intergalactic trips with a well-endowed blonde alien who "looked twenty-five but was more than 500 years old." She had come to Earth, said Menger, "to help." Far more startling to anyone familiar with the plot of *Invaders From Mars* was that Menger one day had taken his twelve-year-old son, Robert, to a pasture near their house to see a UFO and its crew. Robert Menger was dying of brain cancer, and he couldn't see the spacemen, he told his father. Angered that his son didn't believe him, Howard Menger smacked the boy.

Just as the Roswell incident was gaining momentum, in 1986 a remake of *Invaders From Mars* came out, directed by Tobe Hooper, the man behind the *Texas Chainsaw Massacre* movies. At 102 minutes, the remake was almost thirty minutes longer than the woefully short original. But it was only one fifth as good.

The new *Invaders From Mars* appears less like an updated version than a ripoff of other movies. A boy still watches a UFO land in the hill beyond his house. Earthlings still get neck implants from the visitors. The military (Marines, this time) still come to the rescue. In the newer model, the Martians look like rabid hogs and they travel in a spaceship that resembles a boulder with windows.

In an attempt to raise the 1953 version, the 1986 version falls all over itself by stealing parts from other movies. David's father has clandestine meetings with strangers (*Invasion of the Body Snatchers*, 1956, '78); David's teacher swallows live rodents (the 1985 television mini-series *V*); and David's biology class studies frog dissection (*E.T., The Extraterrestrial*).

None of the tension in the '53 version appears in the '86 one. Indeed, after getting zapped by the Martians, David's father, played by Timothy Bottoms, is far too sweet to put fear into anyone. He doesn't raise his hand at his son and barely raises his voice. The sexual tension seems watered down when the viewer realizes that the nurse (Karen Black) in this movie is in real life the mother of David (Hunter Carson).

There's much screaming and yelling, David ray-guns a tunnel to escape from of the cave, and the best line comes from Colonel Fielding's character who has been promoted and given a new last name. "The Marines have no qualms," barks the general as he leads his troops up the sandy hill, "about killing Martians!"

The thievery of *Invaders From Mars* continues. In *One West Waikiki*, a cheesy 1994 TV series, Cheryl Ladd plays a disturbed doctor who has implants in the back of her neck. Same with agent Dana Scully on a 1995 episode of *The X-Files*. *Target Earth*, a 1998 made-for-TV movie, features Earthlings that have been abducted by aliens over the years and surgically fixed with a neck chip that will be activated on the alien version of D-Day.

The Roswell Rules—lab techs, G.I.'s with mortar launchers, and a strong moral—may be *Invaders From Mars*' greatest legacy years later. Those rules can be evidenced as recently as the mid-1990s, in *Species*, which has the requisite radar tower, sterile suits, aggressive soldiers and a Don't-Mess-With-Mother-Nature message. But more often than not it was during the fifties that the Roswell Rules served as guidelines for movie after movie. Take *It Conquered the World* (1956), for example, which surely ranks as one of the worst movies ever put on video. Made by Roger Corman, it starred Peter Graves, a veteran of interplanetary creature films (*Killers From*

Space, Red Planet Mars). The first two words spoken in *It Conquered the World* are "Unidentified object." The line is delivered by a woman who is studying a radar screen and wearing a lab coat. The alien in *It Conquered the World* resembles an enormous kumquat and emits little winged offspring that appear to be bats. The visitors are from Venus and they do not come in peace.

It Conquered the World, which went straight to drive-in theaters, copies both *The Day the Earth Stood Still* and *Invaders From Mars*, and perhaps that is the finest compliment anyone can give the subterranean-budgeted, black-and-white quickie. When the Venusian veggie gets upset on Earth all electricity goes on the blink, all clocks stop. When the alien in *It Conquered the World* wants to control the minds of Earthlings, he has his small, bat-like birds bite humans—*in the back of the neck*. At the end of *It Conquered the World*, a deeply worried Peter Graves moralizes, "There is hope, but it has to come from inside, from man himself."

The moral of Roswell, of course, is this: when the government says something didn't happen, man has hope. Hope that something *did* happen, and that it was covered up. Hope that that cover-up will never actually be exposed because, after all, people, like moviegoers, need something to fantacize about, and to keep believing in, often through the price of a single admission ticket.

chapter 8

Setting Sail in the Solar System

"My barbecue grill was spotted over Roswell, New Mexico."
— *Home Improvement*, 1997

DROP THE LASER, LOUIE.
Though nobody muttered that Bogie-like line in either
Captain Video or *Forbidden Planet*, those two very different dramas
of the 1950s featured protagonists who packed on their hips the
heat of ray guns. Not only did both creations have a large influence
on outer-space entertainment for years to come, but each was a
byproduct of the Roswell residue.

If *The Day the Earth Stood Still* and *Invaders From Mars* provided
inspiration to science-fiction films of the 1950s, *Captain Video* and
Forbidden Planet provided it to the sixties, seventies, eighties, and
onward. Unlike *The Day* and *Invaders*, *Captain Video* and *Forbidden Planet* were not about aliens arriving on this planet, but about
humans going to another planet. Nonetheless, a legitimate line
can be drawn from what may have happened at Roswell to what
did happen on *Captain Video* and *Forbidden Planet*.

The cathode ray tube gave off a tiny, primitive glow when *Captain Video and His Video Rangers*, as the show was properly known,
premiered June 27, 1949, only a little less than two years after the

Roswell incident. Televised live on Channel 5 out of New York City by the DuMont Network, *Captain Video* ran five nights a week, thirty minutes per evening. The show came on in New Mexico via KOB-TV in Albuquerque at 5:30 P.M., and if you had a strong enough antenna, you could pick it up in Roswell. Portraying a homecooked version of life in the heavens, the program for six years magnetized America's youth as no other TV series had. Indeed, *Captain Video* caused many families to buy their first television sets. And what a great name! Not only did the show's title have a ring of authority, but it seemed to stand for everything about the brand-new medium. *Captain Video* was the first science-fiction program on television. The good captain, played for most of the run of the show by a stolid, sharp-featured, stentorian-toned actor named Al Hodge, was the Lone Ranger of the universe, TV's first asteroid-dodging hero. Captain Video roamed the stars in the spaceship *Galaxy* while at the same time he maintained "truth, justice, and freedom," the sort of ideals pledged years later in the Roswell-aroused movie *Independence Day*.

Integrity and honor have long played significant roles in interplanetary experiences, starting with Roswell, which surely served as a model for Hollywood. Mack Brazel, the ranch worker who came upon the debris field allegedy left by a UFO, refused to talk about it years later, even when heaped with ridicule. "He had given his word to the Air Force that he wouldn't say a thing," recalls Brazel's son, Bill, who lives in Capitan, New Mexico. "He wouldn't even talk about it to me and I know that bothered him." When Helen Benson, the character played by actress Patricia Neal in *The Day the Earth Stood Still*, finds out her beau Tom Stevens (Hugh Marlowe) has deceived her in order to turn in the alien Klaatu, Helen won't have anything to do with Stevens. And when Roy Neary, the power-station engineer played by actor Richard Dreyfuss in Steven Spielberg's *Close Encounters of the Third Kind*, realizes no one wants to hear that he's had contact with a UFO, it's as if his word has been invalidated.

As Wagner's stirring overture to "The Flying Dutchman" heralded the start of each *Captain Video* in William Tellish fashion, as every Bosco-gulping kid in the country grew still with anticipation, viewers were put on alert that Captain Video—"*Caaap-TAAAAN Vid-DEEEOOO*"—was the "Master of Space! Guardian of the Safety of the World! Hero of Science!"

But who really was Captain Video? A scientific genius, for one. Self-appointed, dressed in an Eisenhower jacket not unlike those worn in 1947 by Roswell Army Air Field personnel, with a lightning bolt stitched across the front, and pants bloused into jack boots, he took it upon himself as a private citizen to ensure that things went well throughout space. The sheriff of the solar system. Operating from a secret mountaintop headquarters, sometime in the twenty-first or twenty-second century, Captain Video controlled a vast network of "Video Rangers" as well as an impressive arsenal of futuristic weaponry of his own invention. His sidekick was the The Ranger, played by Don Hastings, a young Robin to Video's Batman. The *Galaxy* was a sleek, silvery rocket in the standard form of the 1950s—it was bullet-shaped and blasted off vertically in an extension of the V-2, a design shaped by Roswell's own Robert Goddard.

Mook the Moon Man, Nargola, Hing Foo Seeng, Kul of Eos, Dr. Clysmok, Dahoumie, and the godawful Dr. Pauli, an evil beyond imagination who often battled Video disintegrator gun for disintegrator gun, rotated as the Captain's adversaries. The bad guys came from such planets as Thantos or Quark or, simply, "out there." Jack Klugman, Tony Randall, and Ernest Borgnine were a few of the actors who suited up as villains. Typically madmen with bulging eyes, they bore certain resemblances to what some witnesses had "seen" in Roswell.

To fight the assorted meanies, Video and the Ranger would often reach for the Opticom Scillometer; the Atomic Rifle; the Cosmic Ray Vibrator; or the Radio Scillograph. Also coming in handy were the Remote Tele-Carrier, which could spy on anyone; the Mango

Radar Screen, which could be beamed to any place on Earth and reveal what was going on there; and the Astro-Viewer, which could focus on distant stars.

Gadgetry has always enjoyed a place in discussions of Roswell. The control panel inside the saucer that supposedly crashed there is frequently described as having more buttons than a coat factory. Technospeak is part of the Roswell lore as well. Here's researcher Don Berliner on the Roswell spaceship: "Some reports describe two tabs, located at the rear and symmetrical about the axis of flight motion . . . the discs oscillate laterally while flying along, which could be snaking . . . one observation indicates that the fuel may be throttled, which would indicate a liquid rocket engine."

Rarely was anyone ever killed outright on *Captain Video*; even the crazed Dr. Pauli managed to come back from the dead at least four times. More often than not characters were just left stunned silly or paralyzed stiffer than wallboard. Captain Video and the Ranger couldn't take things for granted, however. Dr. Pauli had his own personal gunrack. It included a Trisonic Compensator, which could curve bullets around a house; a Barrier of Silence, which could cut out all noise; and a Cloak of Invisibility, which could make almost anything disappear.

That robots may have made a rendezvous in Roswell in 1947 has repeatedly been theorized and surely the most terrifying piece of machinery to appear on *Captain Video* was I Tobor ("Robot I" spelled backward). An amiable, indestructible machine, I Tobor helped Captain Video police the Milky Way. Still, every once in a while Tobor would be taken captive by a beautiful villainess named Atar, and programmed to "get Captain Video."

DuMont was a fence-rail poor network, forever a fourth-stringer, and *Captain Video* was a prime example of how DuMont labored diligently to cut costs wherever possible. *Captain Video*'s sets were either a wobbly, dark-painted cardboard or a backdrop of black velvet studded with cheap sequins, which regularly fell off. The control panel knobs on the *Galaxy* looked for all the world like Army surplus dials. The Opticom Scillometer was a sure double for a radiator pipe, with bolts attached. And then there was I Tobor. He was really nothing more than a cylindrical mass of cardboard and cloth with hooks for hands and a window in front out of which zoomed death rays, or so viewers were told.

Writer Bruce Rux says sci-fi silliness and escapist fantasy such as television's *Captain Video* and the movies' *Fire Maidens From Outer Space* (1956), in which astronauts landing on the thirteenth moon of Jupiter face a bevy of nubile females eager for husbands, were all part of a conspiracy in the late-1940s and fifties between Hollywood and the government. The disinformation plan, according to Rux, was to push the public's attention away from thinking too much about what might have happened at Roswell, and to instead get people to laugh over the idea that anything like space travel and aliens *could* happen.

Rux's theory is intriguing. However, most kids didn't mind the inanity of productions such as *Captain Video*, didn't object to the shortcomings, didn't seem to notice them, in fact. The program was a giant success, even as it struggled mightily to get by on a reported budget of thirty dollars a week. So loyal were young viewers that they flooded DuMont with letters asking how to be a Video Ranger. With the same lust displayed by today's adults when they spot a "I Crashed in Roswell" T-shirt for sale, youngsters in the fifties begged for a *Captain Video* secret decoder ring, or pleaded with their parents to get them a space helmet. (The ring cost twenty-five cents and a Post cereal box top; the helmet, a dollar with a Power House candy bar wrapper). Even big people sought those premiums. When Ed Norton of *The Honeymooners*, another extremely popular TV show of the time, in Roswell and elsewhere, bought a television set jointly with his downstairs neighbor, Ralph Kramden, Norton grew wildly excited: he was a Ranger Third Class in the Captain Video Space Academy. One night Norton showed up at the Kramdens' apartment wearing on his noggin a bubble-topped fishbowl, complete with flapping antennae. Kramden, however, wanted to watch something else that evening, and soon the loud and familiarly exasperating Jackie Gleason vs. Art Carney argument ensued.

Grown-ups may have chuckled at the crudeness of *Captain Video*'s sets and the fakery of the show's staging, but *CV* managed to win numerous adult admirers. And for good reason. After most episodes, Captain Video himself would appear on screen and, issuing words in a voice that sailed straight and true to every rumpus room coast to coast, the Cap'n delivered to his young troops tips on the value of tolerance, fair play, and personal integrity, morals that reassured Americans in the early years of the Cold War.

The popularity of *Captain Video* paralleled the popularity of television. By 1952, when the show was at its zenith, there were nineteen million TV sets in the country and one thousand new stores selling those sets opened each month. *Captain Video* managed to attract scripts from a number of famous writers, such as science-fiction luminary Damon Knight. In time, though, DuMont's battle to survive proved too costly. The floundering network pulled the plug on the series in the spring of 1955, and DuMont itself soon shut down.

Captain Video endured as a progenitor of numerous space shows of the 1950s, including *Space Patrol* and *Tom Corbett-Space Cadet*. Yet all were pale imitations of the real *Captain*. *Star Trek*, which arrived in 1966 and eventually developed a charmed life of its own that continues even today as the Number One cult show, has a good portion of its roots in *Captain Video*. *Star Trek*'s creator and producer, Gene Roddenberry, learned to write for early episodic television when *CV* ruled the land. Like *Captain Video*, *Star Trek* has villains—Klingons and Romulans—and a likeable robotic persona in Mr. Spock. *Quark*, which debuted on NBC in 1978, also offered a salute to *Captain Video* by taking one of the show's planets as its title. The scary, lurching automaton of *The Day the Earth Stood Still*, the scrap-metal figure of "Bubble-headed Booby" used in television's campy *Lost in Space,* and even Rosie the robot maid in *The Jetsons* can be tracked to *Captain Video.*

Though it boasted signature lunch boxes and board games, *Star Trek* was not the first TV show to market itself to its viewers through endorsements. *Captain Video* takes that honor, thanks to the promotion of a wide range of products that included dishes, toy rockets, comic books, and even bedspreads.

James Caddigan, creator and producer of *Captain Video,* once told an interviewer that the popularity of *CV* could be explained in the way a flying saucer grabs the everyday person. Caddigan said that traveling through space will be possible and that "We may soon be visited by other beings if we haven't been already."

Television, that most powerful of popular culture mediums, seemed eager to dispatch to America's living rooms *anything* about spacecraft. All through the sixties stand-up comedian Bill Dana, portraying sad-faced, heavily-accented Jose Jimenez, proclaimed, "I want to be an astronaut." *Lost in Space* (1967) featured a Swiss Family Robinson-like clan that wandered the heavens in the far-off year of 1997 and, without oxygen masks, continually landed on a planet that each week looked the same as the last.

Almost twenty-five years after *CV* left the scene, the show reappeared, this time on the front page of *The New York Times.* On March 18, 1979, Al Hodge, the actor who had helped to make the television program famous, was found dead in a rundown hotel room in midtown New York City. Broke and alone except for a few crinkled photographs he had saved of himself as Captain Video with a ray gun, Hodge was sixty-six.

The news stunned many Americans. Hodge at one point had a fan following as formidable as another 1950s' television idol, Superman. Hodge's death shows that when a popular culture figure falls, such as George Reeves, the actor who played TV's *Superman,* and who died of a self-inflicted gunshot wound in 1959, he often falls hard. In the early 1950s, Hodge, who had been the voice of the *Green Hornet* on radio, was a national hero. In his *CV* heyday, Hodge had told reporters that he proudly sent his advance scripts to his nine-year-old daughter in Cincinnati so she could follow his live perfomances line by line. Hodge never made a slip-up, his daughter remembered years afterward. Hodge loved the role, loved the adulation and the responsibility. Bursting with great pride, he would regularly take helicopter trips to suburban New York City communities to make personal appearances.

But when *Captain Video* ended, Hodge's career apparently did, too. He appeared in a couple of TV shows—*Alfred Hitchcock Presents* and *Naked City*—and then he went to Hollywood to try to break into the movies. He failed miserably at that venture. "I'm too damned typecast as *Captain Video*," he complained to friends. He returned to New York City and wound up selling real estate on Long Island. Eventually, things grew worse as Hodge went through his third marriage and began to drink heavily. He picked up a job as a bank guard and then worked in security for Cartier's, the jewelry store. As the drinking continued, his health deteriorated. Hodge tried to find work on TV commercials, but typecasting again prevented him from getting a foothold there, too. By 1970, Hodge had sunk deep into alcoholism. He tried to remain upbeat and acquaintances remembered him from that period as mostly dapper and optimistic—as if the one big part he wanted was right around the corner. But he never got it, never got another acting job. In 1975, Hodge, his daughter said, "disappeared." In truth, he moved into a nine-dollar-a-night single room in Manhattan and began to drink himself into oblivion. Death was said due to chronic bronchitis and severe emphsyma, but others knew the real cause. Al Hodge, the great Captain Video, the guardian of the universe, the preserver of justice, truth and freedom, had died of a broken heart.

Some scholars might try to make a correlation between Hodge and Jesse Marcel Sr., the Roswell-based intelligence officer. According to the movie *Roswell*, Marcel, long after the 1947 incident, was filled with resentment and regret that he been forced by the Army Air Force into agreeing that what had been found was not from outer space, but was rather, a weather balloon. However, Marcel had simply obeyed orders and went along with what his superiors told him to do that week in July. By all accounts, Marcel never was bitter over what had transpired—only baffled.

A year after *Captain Video and His Video Rangers* exited the little screen, one of the most significant space films ever made opened on the big screen. Like *Captain Video*, *Forbidden Planet* owes much to the nature of the Roswellian era that preceded it. In turn, *Forbidden Planet* inspired a constellation of space films and shows that followed—from *Alien* to *Star Wars* to the never-ending continuum of *Star Trek*.

Forbidden Planet was based on a story titled *Fatal Planet*, a loose adaption of Shakespeare's *The Tempest*. A great surge of interest in science fiction in the early fifties, emanating from flying saucer spottings in the late 1940s, sent a steady stream of sci-fi scripts to the offices of Hollywood producers and studio heads. Most of these scripts were alarmingly lousy. But not *Forbidden Planet*. For the magician Prospero, the movie's creators substituted Dr. Morbius, a bit of of a mad scientist; Prospero's daughter, Miranda, a young woman who knows only one man—her father—became Altaira; as the sprite Ariel, there was Robby the Robot; and as Caliban, moviemakers dreamed up a marveously flamboyant monster. Unwittingly concocted by Dr. Morbius, this sometimes invisible, sometimes red menace, resembled a cross between the Metro-Goldwyn-Mayer lion and a Japanese sumo wrestler. Viewed these days the monster has similarities to the cartoon character known as the Tasmanian Devil. But a closer look reveals the monster has a goatee—just as did Walter Pidgeon, the actor who played Morbius. More important, the monster comes from Morbius's own id, from the feelings he has for his daughter.

Not surprisingly, DNA found in *Forbidden Planet* can be found in *Captain Video*. Robby the Robot was an I Tobor update, albeit a far more sophisticated, infinitely more intelligent automaton. Indeed, Robby, one the first legitimate robots to appear in movies, speaks "187 languages, along with various dialects and sub-tongues." And like *Captain Video*, *Forbidden Planet* took place in the early part of the 22nd century—or more precisely, 2257, a time, according to Les Tremayne, the movie's narrator whose sotto voice seems to come from another solar system, "when men and women landed on the moon in rocket ships."

Those men in the rocket ships of *Forbidden Planet* were crew members of United Planets cruiser C57-D, which in reality did not resemble a rocket ship at all but was instead a dead ringer for the quintessential, sombrero-shaped flying saucer. On the screen, good guys were riding a UFO!

Not surprisingly, *Forbidden Planet* played to a full house when it opened during the summer of 1956 in Roswell's Plains Theater (now "scientifically cooled"). Roswell audiences had had their appetites whetted for the movie through a plate of science-fiction hors d'oeuvres. Earlier in the year The Plains had featured *Target Earth*, starring Richard Denning. "Raw panic!" cried the ads. "The robots are coming!" That film was followed by *On the Threshold of Space*, starring Guy Madison. Ads for *Threshold*, which was filmed in nearby Alamogordo and told the story of early-day space flight preparations, said, "Here are the men who defy speed, space and human endurance . . . in rocket sleds, balloon gondolas, and ejection seats!" Next up was *Earth vs. The Flying Saucers*: "See New York, London, Paris, Moscow shudder under saucer attacks."

A viewer today can see a great deal of *Star Trek* within *Forbidden Planet*, and vice versa, right down to the the six-gun blasters the crews carry, the comfy executive chairs they sit on, and the familiar gray outfits they wear. Thus, it comes as no shock to learn that Gene Roddenberry as a kid in El Paso, Texas, used to read *Astounding Stories*, the magazine where the idea for *Forbidden Planet* originated. "The Man Trap," the premiere episode of *Star Trek*, took a page from *Forbidden Planet*—and Roswell. An archaeologist finds the sole survivor on a planet to be a creature with suction-cup fingertips—digits resembling those described by Roswell eyewitnesses.

There's more: just as the crew of *Star Trek* gets "beamed up," the crew of the C-57D is similarly transported. A handsome captain and a sharp-tongued doctor are on board both the Starship *Enterprise* and C-57D. What's more, *Forbidden Planet* was the first science-fiction movie to feature a military space organization, the raison d'etre of *Star Trek*. Indeed, both shows adopted contemporary Navy terms, ranks, and jargon to give the characters a closer, more familiar connnection to the audience: Aye-aye, Skipper . . . Starboard ten degrees . . . All hands square away to decelerate. Finally, the C-57D of *Forbidden Planet* had its own gadgetry, more technical than anything seen thus far in films: a gyro stabilizer, a klystron monitor, and a viewplate activator.

It wasn't just *Star Trek* that paid close attention to *Forbidden Planet*. The haunted house metaphor seen in the 1979 space horror *Alien* owes a big debt of gratitude to *Forbidden Planet*. When the hideous and stealthlike id one night slips inside C-57D, no one in the rocket ship knows the monster is there until it has chewed up a few of the crew. When *Dr. Who*, the wildly inventive British-made, stellar-voyaging TV series that began in the sixties, needed a villain, they found one in "the brain of Morbius." Finally, C-3PO of *Star Wars*'s fame certainly mimicked genial, eager-to-please Robby the Robot.

Robby the Robot, surely the real star of *Forbidden Planet*, appeared as a delightful barrel of gauges and rotors. His purring tones belonged to Marvin Miller, the familiar voice of the 1950s TV series *The Millionaire*. Robby could, it seemed, synthesize anything from scratch, including enough bourbon to drown New Orleans. (Similar liquor-inspired laughs show up in *E.T.* when the alien gets tipsy from too many beers). To younger moviegoers, Robby was a pop culture version of the Beanie Baby doll. Robby, who served as the role model for all the lovable movie robots in years to come, along with other props from *Forbidden Planet*, turned up later on such television shows as *The Twilight Zone* and *Lost in Space*. And why not? Machinelike creations, admitted Dr. Robert I. Sarbacher, once a member of the so-called ultra-secret investigative MJ-12 in the 1940s, might well have been the aliens the Army encountered at Roswell. Thus, Robby joined Gort of *The Day the Earth Stood Still* to become filmdom's two best-known robots.

The mission of C-57D was to reach Earth-like Altair-IV, which some twenty years before was the crash site of a scientific space expedition. The voyage to Altair-IV, a journey deep into hyperspace, required 378 days. Prior to *Forbidden Planet* no film had ever left Earth so far behind; indeed, the idea of interstellar travel was reasonably new in 1956. So how did the rocket travel so quickly? Using something called "quanto-gravetitic hyperdrive," C-57D shot through space at the speed of light. Thankfully, an astrogator, or navigator, kept the ship on the right course.

When the crew from C-57D arrives at Altair-IV, Dr. Morbius repeatedly tells them to go back, warns members that they are not welcome. It seems that Morbius, played with a good dose of urbane angst by Pidgeon, and his daughter (a fetching, miniskirted, barefoot Anne Francis), are the planet's only residents, all that is left of the earlier scientific expedition. The crew of C-57D eventually learns from Morbius of a fascinating group of people called the Krell, an extinct superintelligent race that many centuries before inhabited Altair-IV. The Krell built a magnificient underground machine to materialize mental energy, forgetting that doing so would also unleash the evil that exists in the mind. It's the id that has plagued Morbius—who has become almost a Krell himself—that extinguished the earlier expedition and that attacks the crew of the C-57D.

The *Krell* was not some randomly invented name. In many stories that have evolved from Roswell over time, particularly those rumors that have to do with MJ-12, the word *Krlll*—with no vowels and three l's—has frequently been explained as an "ebe" or extraterrestrial biological entity, picked up in the New Mexico desert and taken to the oh-so-clandestine Area 51 in Nevada.

Directed by Fred M. Wilcox, *Forbidden Planet* was well-received by critics. *Time* magazine called it "nifty" and added in typically inscrutable *Time*-ese fashion, "The special effects should convince any wavering space cadet that it's ether or."

Forbidden Planet is still considered the best of sci-fi interstellar productions of the 1950s, far and away superior to a slew that surfaced during that decade, a collection that ranged from *Radar Men From the Moon* (1952) to *Robot Monster* (1953) to *Duel in Space* (1954) to *Invasion of the Saucer Men* (1957). If 1951's *The Day the Earth Stood Still* ignited the fire of science-fiction films, *Forbidden Planet* turned that fire into an awesome blaze. Many critics rank *Forbidden Planet* on a par with *2001: A Space Odyssey* (1968). Indeed, until *2001* no science-fiction film was as expensive, ambitious, or as visually stirring as *Forbidden Planet*. Or as cerebral. In *Forbidden Planet*, viewers are taken deep into space only to confront what is deepest in themselves—secret impulses and desires usually not spoken of. The movie presents a fascinating and delicate handling of incest, one of the first films to do so. When Morbius feels the classic threat to his daughter from the young male crewmen, it's time for the monstrous id to be released. The sets of *Forbidden Planet*—green skies and pink deserts—and the chilling electronic tonalities—periodic whirring and whining—are memorable. So is the Walt Disney-developed monster, who originally was conceptualized as being completely invisible. Even the science is accurate. The C-57D saucer/cruiser travels at .3896 of light speed, which is rightly said to be roughly 2.6 million miles per hour. And that deer and those tigers: where did they come from? Instead of ignoring that obvious question, the movie tells viewers the animals came from a trip the Krell took to Earth, millions of years before.

Still, *Forbidden Planet* is not without shortcomings, as are so many science-fiction creations of the fifties. One reviewer complained that the movie's makers should have used Shakespeare's language. Indeed, some of the dialogue, particularly when delivered by the sluggish crew of C-57D, contains more lead than a pound of paint:

> "Dr. Morbius, a scientific find of this magnitude has got to be taken under United Planet supervision. No one man can monopolize it."
>
> "It must have been renewing its molecular structure from one microsecond to another."
>
> "We young men have been shut up in hyperspace for well over a year."

Stiff lines aside, *Forbidden Planet* offers romance, humor, and suspense and yet it is ultimately a thinking-person's movie, an intellectually challenging experience, and that's what truly gives it staying power. The visit to the wonders of the Krell and their underground maze of machinery is a marvelous trip. Going inside the machineworks is like going inside the mind of a planet. A thermal nuclear furnace lies below everything, the purpose of the entire complex is a mystery that even Morbius has not yet solved. One thing is certain, however: the monster is a projection of Morbius's own mind, fed by the power of the giant Krell machine. It's that awful id that eventually destroys Morbius and his planet.

As *Captain Video* did, *Forbidden Planet* left behind a peculiar entry in the history of popular culture, albeit a much happier note than actor Al Hodge's tragic demise. The planet Altair-IV and Dr. Morbius' s daughter, Altaira, are named for the the brightest star in the constellation, Aquila. Almost twenty years after the film was released, the name Altaira was given to the world's first personal computer.

Built in Albuquerque in 1975 by former Air Force engineer and film buff Ed Roberts, with a software assist from a young Harvard dropout named Bill Gates, the Altair personal computer appeared a full two-and-a-half years before the Apple. The Altair was a shoebox-shaped device without a keyboard or display terminal and it worked from a series of switches in a binary language. The Altair came in assembly kits and Roberts's company, MITS, shipped more than 5,000 pc's in 1975. Putting the thing together, however, required great patience, a steady hand and a good soldering gun. With competition suddenly on the horizon, Roberts eventually sold his company in 1977 and he entered medical school. Later, Roberts said his mission had been to get the computer into the hands of people to prevent the possibility of the grim 1984 forseen by George Orwell.

A fate far worse than being sold came to the other Altair, the planet, once inhabited by the Krell. As Altaira and the crew of the C-57D watch from space while the doomed orb explodes into billions of particles, a crewman provides a eulogy in a voice heavily shaded with the intonations and wisdom of someone who has been ruminating over the meaning of Roswell. "We are after all," observes the crewman, "not God."

Captain Video resurrected the Roswell incident in the minds of those who had buried memories of it. By intrinsically prodding viewers with the idea that crazy robots and goofy aliens could be out there—that Roswell *could* have existed—the show became acceptable. In the same manner, sudden recollections of the Roswell incident, flashbacks, if you will, told audiences that *Forbidden Planet* was not so far-fetched. The movie was smart, and it was smart people, after all, believers have decided, who camouflaged Roswell, who tried to hide it from the human consciousness, and who ultimately failed.

afterword

"Roswell . . . it won't go away. Why not?"
—*Larry King Live,* 1997

WHATEVER MAY HAVE HAPPENED AT ROSWELL possesses
the kind of staying power achieved perhaps by only one other
popular culture icon: Elvis Presley. Roswell remains with us, as
does Elvis, for many of the same reasons. Though their legion can
be sophisticated and well-educated, followers of both phenomena
generally belong to a cross-section of America that likely wouldn't
buy Danish-modern furniture or read Simone de Beauvoir. For
the most part, the true believers come from provincial, small-town
America. The Roswell incident then could not have happened in,
say, Atlanta or Minneapolis. It had to occur in an undersized community, somewhat remote, but eager to show off the Stars and
Stripes on any holiday. Elvis has a place in that America. "HONK
IF YOU SAW ELVIS," says the bumper sticker that could well be
spotted along Roswell's Main Street.

People want to believe in Roswell, just as they want to believe
in Elvis, because Roswell, like Elvis, represents a comforting dis-
traction in a world that often is plagued by sorrow. What's more,
the alternative to Roswell—to Elvis—devotees sense, is bound to

be far less entertaining, far less filled with wonder or even, wackiness.

Roswell and Elvis share this also: steadfast, unable-to-be-swayed zealots. The same claimants who say Roswell happened in 1947, say that Elvis did not die in 1977. The same people who swear aliens from Roswell are stashed in a Fridgidaire, are dead-certain that Elvis currently is ringing up two tins of Copenhagen at a Stop 'n' Go in Nacogdoches, Texas. (Elvis never would be clerking at a supermarket in, for instance, Seattle.)

The same worshipers who won't let Roswell fade away are those who don't want to see Elvis completely disappear, either. Indeed, Elvis CDs continue to fill up shopping carts, mutton-chopped Elvis impersonators turn up at every talent show, and Graceland, Elvis's Memphis home, needs a security force to keep the wave of visitors in check. Though crowds in Roswell have slowed since the fiftieth anniversary, the annual UFO festival still has broad appeal, while the incident itself seldom fails to earn a mention in any new piece of material that touches on UFOs.

Therefore, it isn't surprising to learn that Elvis Presley believed in the extraterrestrial, and that fact has won him great admiration among the Roswell dedicated. As a kid, Elvis's favorite comic book was *Captain Marvel*, and as an adult he liked to wear costumes that, like Marvel's, featured lightning bolts down the front. At one point, Elvis reportedly gave his wife, Priscilla, fits by raving for hours about the "powerful forces" that were pulling stars through the galaxies.

In 1966, Elvis cemented for eternity his exalted status among E.T. congregants. Late one night that year, while standing in the back yard of his home in Bel Air, California, Elvis said he glanced heavenward and saw a UFO. What is surprising: that Elvis once saw Roswell. It happened in 1955, and the little-known event marks a historic moment in the annals of popular culture, for it truly was the intersection of two larger-than-life attractions that have continued to glitter long after the curtain has gone down.

On February 14, 1955, Elvis was barely twenty years old, an unheralded and unsequined rockabilly singer from the Deep South. He had not yet joined forces with his celebrated manager, Colonel Tom Parker, nor had he even recorded a hit song. Elvis was touring that winter with a Grand Ole Opry group and on Valentine's Day night the group, headed by country-western star Hank Snow, played, according to an advertisement in the *Roswell Record*, "two big shows" at the North Junior High School auditorium. The concert was a benefit for the Roswell Fire Department, and tickets sold for a dollar in advance, $1.25 at the door. As might be expected, Snow received top billing for the performances. The next name on the marquee belonged to the Duke of Paducah, followed by the Rainbow Ranch Boys. Then, finally, Elvis Presley, "star of the Louisiana Hayride." It's unclear if anyone took note of Elvis's appearance and the *Roswell Record* did not bother to review the concert.

Years later, Elvis and Roswell tied a much stronger knot through the sale of souvenirs and memorabilia. Many Roswell UFO items feature the King of Rock 'n' Roll, with guitar in hand—getting into a spaceship, or bearing the superimposed head of an alien, or crooning to a saucer in the sky. Like Elvis has done, Roswell will continue to flourish as long as small-town, flag-waving values thrive in America. Elvis, after all, served proudly in the U.S. Army, while Roswell served for twenty-five years as the home of a vital military installation. Elvis stands as a monument to Americana, as, in a way, does Roswell, and it's difficult to tear down monuments.

Whatever may have happened in Roswell has not only endured over time, but over distance as well. Not long after I did the initial work on this book, I moved to eastern Europe where I spent a year as a Fulbright Scholar teaching journalism at the University of Bucharest. On occasion I would travel about Romania to give a lecture and sometimes my talks would be about Roswell. Initially I wasn't sure what Romanians thought about the extraterrestrial. Indeed, during a visit to a university in the city of Sibiu,

I was met by a sea of empty expressions when I talked of space aliens. Then I mentioned the word Roswell, the only place on Earth where a spaceship supposedly was snatched up by a government apparently consumed with secretiveness. For emphasis, I repeated the word: *Roswell*. Suddenly, a voice from the back of the lecture hall shouted something. "Pardon?" I answered. Then came the spectator's cry again: "*Dosarele X.*"

Doe-suh-rell-ay Icks, known elsewhere as *The X-Files*, was, I learned that day, the name of one of the most watched television shows in Romania—along with, curiously, *The Streets of San Francisco* and a Brazilian soap opera. Of greater significance: someone on *The X-Files* periodically speaks of Roswell, which has helped Roswell to become a buzzword within the UFO community—anywhere. Romanians know Roswell because they know how to turn on the TV.

Oddly, Romania has more in common with Roswell than one would think. Constantin Brancusi, Romania's greatest artist and the father of modern sculpture, created an acclaimed work titled *Mademoiselle Pogany*. So famous is the ovoidal bust that it decorates one side of the most circulated piece of currency in the country, the 500 lei bill. Of greater significance: upon close inspection, *Mademoiselle Pogany* bears an uncanny resemblance to the slanty-eyed, frying pan-faced alien of Roswell.

For many years, Romanians did not think much of Dracula, *their* country's celebrated icon. Dracula was a folk myth, Romanians countered, built around the story of Vlad the Impaler, the nasty, fifteenth century ruler of Wallachia, and fictionalized four centuries later by an Irishman, Bram Stoker. Stoker's novel definitely was not part of Romania's history, the argument went. Yes, there is a Transylvania, but it's a place that has absolutely nothing to do with blood-sucking, stake-in-the-heart tales of vampires. Still, visitors to Romania continued to ask about Dracula, in the same manner that visitors once asked Roswell about aliens. Is that really his castle over there on that hill? Can someone really have teeth that long? Where are all the bats?

Romanians finally realized, as Roswellians had some time before, that doubt is no reason to turn down money. Indeed, Romania's poor economy resembled Roswell's during pre-UFO days. Revenues were desperately needed in both places. When Romania tourist officials noticed that visitors were wandering about, hungry for peeks into supposedly historic caskets, the scramble began to feed that hunger. Sounding a great deal like Roswell's Chamber of Commerce director, Romania's Minister of Tourism told *The Times* of London, "If people want hands coming out of coffins, we'll give it to them." Promoters quickly set up Dracula tours across Transylvania, much like Roswell Crash-Site tours. I spent a Halloween sightseeing at Dracula's lair, the famed fortress known as Castle Bran, where allegedly Vlad the Impaler once slept. At the foot of the castle, Roswell-like souvenir shops sell instead of an alien's face Vlad's menacing visage on everything from charm bracelets to walking sticks. Moreover, Dracula T-shirts can now be bought across the countryside, restaurants and bars with Dracula motifs pop up every week, and fang-embellished canvas tote bags, ceramic mugs, and wooden dolls flood the marketplace. A Dracula theme park planned for downtown Bucharest was announced, and then apparently put on hold.

As long as people have faith in Dracula, as long as they're certain that Elvis breathes, they will honor Roswell. And yet, just when you think Roswell might have gone away for good, back it comes, in every manner of popular culture. A 1998 television commercial featured a Maytag repairman standing in a very Roswell-like field. Suddenly a UFO drops to the desert floor a washing machine and three aliens. The spaceship's work done, the aliens then fly off. The viewer, however, learns that the washer's stain remover is "out of this world." We also learn the washer's name: The Neptune.

Baseball fans would not have believed it, but Roswell nearly edged out of the sports headlines slugger Mark McGwire's achievement during the 1998 Major League Baseball season. McGwire, of course, was glorified for hitting a record seventy home runs. But the real baseball record, according to statistics-keepers, belonged to an obscure minor leaguer. Joe Bauman played for the Roswell (New Mexico) Rockets in the long-vanished Class C Longhorn League. In 1954, the 6-5, 240-pound Bauman belted an extraordinary seventy-two home runs. He accomplished the feat in 138 games, a rate that would have produced eighty-five of them in a 162-game schedule.

As McGwire surpassed Babe Ruth, and then Roger Maris, for baseball's single-season home run mark, and as he neared his 70th, reporters began calling on Joe Bauman for comments, since his record suddenly seemed in peril. Bauman, in his mid-seventies and retired from running his own gas station in Roswell, still lived in the city. He was modest about his batting mark. "It's a totally different game today," he said.

But reporters couldn't leave the Roswell connection alone. When a writer for *Sports Illustrated* learned that the ball that Bauman hit for his seventy-second home run had once been on display at a museum, but that Bauman had never seen the ball, the writer pointed out that this museum was in Roswell, "near the site of the alleged UFO crash in 1947 . . . you don't suppose?"

Roswell skeptics, such as science-fiction writer Jack Williamson, of neighboring Portales, New Mexico, will always exist, for the climate of popular culture by nature promotes sustainment as well as suspicion. However, even Williamson must have been surprised by an astonishing event that occurred in Portales during mid-1998 and that gave the Roswell incident new energy. On June 13 of that year, a meteor showered the Portales area with rock fragments. Thirty-eight pieces of meteorite were collected over a five-mile stretch in eastern New Mexico, not that far from where a UFO supposedly plowed into the side of a hill. Some of the rocks were several centimeters long. One football-sized rock that slammed into the back yard of Portales art teacher Nelda Wallace, weighed thirty-seven pounds. "There were several booms, then it sounded like a jet plane coming in," Wallace told the Associated Press. The rock made a ten-inch-deep hole. An eleven-pound fragment ripped through a barn roof belonging to Portales farmer Robert Newberry.

Was the shower a sign somehow connected to the Roswell incident? Many adherents of the Roswell story leaped at the notion that, yes, this bombardment from space would truly reveal to doubters the truth about little gray men. On the other hand, scientists held firm. They concurred that the rock from which the fragments came was originally formed 4.6 billion years ago as a cloud of dust balls condensed early in the history of our solar system.

Researchers collected eighty to ninety percent of the meteorite. Nelda Wallace dutifully pried the rock from her yard and carted it to the University of New Mexico Institute of Meteoritics—in a bowling bag. The Portales Valley Meteorite, the name geologists gave the rock, apparently struck the Earth's atmosphere at more than 20,000 miles per hour but was crushed by the increasing air pressure before flying apart. Additional samples of the Portales meteorite, however, still remained in collectors' hands, so a full analysis was not possible. The University of New Mexico Institute of Meteoritics was trying to gather money to buy samples from collectors who, like their neighbors in Roswell, have learned much about the free enterprise system. Indeed, some Portales collectors announced they would only part with their rock—for a price.

So on and on marches the Roswell incident, refueled at irregular intervals by almost any kind of happening. It seems Roswell won't expire because it lives for anyone to pin almost anything on it. In 1997, I wrote a historical article about a B-29 Superfortress, a bomber with a wingspan of almost half a football field and the height of nearly three stories, that had crashed soon after takeoff from Albuquerque's old Kirtland Field.

Twelve men on board were killed in what at the time was the

worst air disaster in New Mexico. The date was January 27, 1947. Officials placed the primary blame of the crash on the failure of the No. 1 engine at takeoff. The flight had been a routine training mission, but because B-29s had once carried atomic bombs, through the years the clandestine nature of the mission seemed to expand and caused investigative sorts to create a link between the plane and the alleged crash of a UFO in Roswell, less than six months away. When I proposed this theory to Roy Bedwell, who had been stationed at Kirtland Field in 1947, he shook his head and looked at me as if I had meteorites lodged in mine.

Roswell lives on because our fascination with space travel lives on. For its new international space station, NASA in early 1998 asked young Internet readers to suggest a name. *Totally Rad Space Place*, *Milky Way Bar Stop*, *Giant Space Thingy*, and *Better Than Mir* were among the thousands of nominations, along with this one: *Roswell North*. John Glenn, America's first man in orbit, became the oldest man in orbit when space shuttle Discovery lifted off in October 1998, atop a blaze of publicity, thirty-six and a half years after Glenn's first rocket ride. Glenn, seventy-seven, came up with the ingenious idea in the mid-1990s of launching a senior citizen to better understand the disorders shared by the elderly on Earth as well as astronauts in space: flabby muscles, brittle bones, weakened immune systems, dizzy spells, and fitful sleep. Not coincidentally, Roswell residents cheered as loud for Glenn's latest heroics as any people in the country, and for good reason. The city, it must be noted, was named in 1998 by *Kiplinger's Personal Finance* magazine as one of the six best places to retire in the nation. The Retirement Services Division of Roswell reports that 22.9 percent of the 47,559 population is older than fifty-five.

More to the point: Glenn took with him on that trip a swatch of fabric from the world's first flying machine, produced by the Wright Brothers in 1903, in Dayton, Ohio. News of Glenn's carry-on item generated a blizzard of letters to various paranormal publications. Why, many letter-writers asked, couldn't Glenn have taken with him something else from Dayton, such as a piece of that spaceship recovered in New Mexico in 1947?

As long as there are questions such as that, questions with no easy answers, Roswell, like Elvis sightings, like Dracula divertissements, will forever have an audience.

credits

sources

BOOKS ABOUT UNIDENTIFIED FLYING OBJECTS are like books about unwanted flabby skin: there is no shortage to choose from. However, UFO works that focused primarily on Roswell and that consistently assisted me were Kevin Randle and Donald Schmitt's *UFO Crash at Roswell* (1991); Stanton Friedman and Don Berliner's *Crash at Corona: the U.S. Military Retrieval and Cover-up of a UFO* (1994); and Philip J. Klass's *The Real Roswell Crashed-Saucer Coverup* (1997).

Other UFO books that drew my attention were: *Close Encounters of the Fourth Kind: Alien Abduction, UFOs, and the Conference at MIT* (1995), by C.D.B. Bryan; *Out There: The Government's Secret Quest for Extraterrestrials* (1990), by Howard Blum; and *Alien Agenda: Investigating the Extraterrestrial Presence Among Us* (1997), by Jim Marrs. Jerome Clark's massive, three-volume *UFO Encyclopedia* (1990–1996), is a marvelous compilation that I reached for regularly.

For a treatment of early-day flying saucer experiences, I liked *The Coming of the Saucer*, by Kenneth Arnold and Ray Palmer, published in 1952. Also helpful was Helen and Bryant Reeve's *Flying Saucer Pilgrimage*, from 1957. The Wisconsin couple traveled 23,000 miles to visit with people who had seen UFOs, including a Mexican chauffeur who told the Reeves he had driven around some alien passengers for several hours—and didn't receive a gratuity.

Anytime I felt overwhelmed by the technology of the field, I turned to a delightful children's text, *How to Catch a Flying Saucer* (1990), by James M.Deem, which has paragraphs such as this one: "Have you ever taken a long drive across the country? You can't go too far before you need to stop for gas or a bathroom or sometimes a repair. Think of UFOs the same way. If they do come from galaxies millions of light-years away, they may need to make a rest stop."

For background on Roswell as a place, no more comprehensive work exists than *Roundup on the Pecos* (1978), by Elvis E. Fleming and Minor S. Huffman. You won't find a word about flying saucers in it, but the information value is unlimited. Starting with prehistoric man, the book covers huge chunks of time and finishes with a fine slice of local genealogy. John C. Sinclair's *Cowboy Riding Country* (1982), especially the first two chapters, contains wonderful portraits of Roswell in the twenties and thirties.

Science Fiction Gold: Film Classics of the Fifties (1979), by Dennis Saleh, and *Science Fiction Films* (1992), by Kate Haycock, served as superb guides to an underappreciated Hollywood genre. *The Great Television Heroes* (1975), by Donald Glut and Jim Harmon, aided my recall of *Captain Video*, while *Ground Zero* (1995), by Kevin J. Anderson, showed me why *The X-Files* and Roswell share much in common.

Hollywood Vs. the Aliens: the Motion Picture Industry's Participation in UFO Disinformation, is not an easy book to locate, even though only published in 1997. Exhaustive but exhilarating, the Bruce Rux project is a wonderful combination of scholarship, theory, and plain fun.

No more authoritative study of Robert Goddard's life exists than Milton Lehman's *This High Man* (1963). Other biographies that I consulted were: *Brando: A Life in Our Times* (1991), by Richard Schickel; *Bob Crosby—World Champion Cowboy* (1966), by Thelma Jones Crosby and Eve Ball; *Wernher von Braun* (1965), by Heather M. David; *H.G. Wells: Desperately Mortal* (1986), by David C. Smith; *Orson Welles, the Rise and Fall of an American Genius* (1985), by Charles Higham; *P.T. Barnum: America's Greatest Showman* (1995), by Philip B. Kunhardt Jr., Philip B. Kunhardt III, and Peter W. Kunhardt; *John Simpson Chisum, Jinglebob King of the Pecos* (1984), by Mary Whatley Clark; *Gene Roddenberry: The Myth and the Man Behind Star Trek* (1994), by Joel Engel; and *Elvis and Me* (1985), by Priscilla Beaulieu Presley, with Sandra Harmon.

Donn Rogosin's *Invisible Men: Life in Baseball's Negro Leagues* (1983) supplied fresh insights about Larry Doby. And Jack Williamson's *Wonder's Child: My Life in Science Fiction* (1984), permitted a thorough inspection of that author's world.

To guide me through the intellectual minefield of social hypotheses, I examined *Mass Media and the Popular Arts* (1983), edited by Fred Rissover and David Birch; *Understanding Popular Culture* (1989), by John Fiske; Susan Sontag's *Against Interpretation and Other Essays* (1966), and Leslie Fiedler's *In Dreams Awake* (1975). Jan Harold Brunvand's *The Vanishing Hitchhiker* (1981) makes a clear case for the need to study tales once heard only around campfires.

Magazines often proved as rewarding as books, for it seemed that every magazine published in 1996 or 1997 featured an article in conjunction with Roswell's UFO incident. *Time, Newsweek, The New Yorker, Forbes, U.S. News & World Report, Popular Mechanics, Popular Science, Entertainment Weekly,* and *UFO Magazine* offered beneficial references. For facts about George van Tassel, the man who gave birth to UFO festivals, I went to issues of *Desert* magazine, from the sixties. For a critique of Whitley Strieber's abduction accounts, I found Thomas M. Disch's 1986 article in *Nation* extremely worthwhile. In the same manner, J.P. Cahn's 1952 exposé in *True* laid bare Frank Scully's reporting of the Aztec incident.

Newsletters from the early 1990s, in particular MUFON's *International UFO Symposium Proceedings*, *The International UFO Reporter*, and *IUR*, filled sizable gaps.

Often considered ephemeral, newspapers, thankfully, live on through microfilm. The *Roswell Daily Record*—in 1947, as well as before and after—reveals an excellent reflection of small-town life in America. *The Washington Post, USA Today, Albuquerque Journal, Albuquerque Tribune, El Paso Times*, and *Arizona Republic* all checked in with constructive reporting on Roswell during 1997. Similarly, that same year a Georgie Anne Geyer syndicated column about the movie *Contact* oozed admirable logic.

Numerous personal interviews went into the mix of this undertaking. Providing me with material I could not have retrieved anywhere else were three terrific subjects: Velma Corley, Domingo Lopez, and Colin McMillan.

Roswell-related events and remarks can be found on video, and I spent many pleasant evenings in front of the VCR. Movies I found particularly useful were:

Abbott and Costello Go to Mars

Alien

Alien Autopsy: Fact or Fiction?

Capricorn One

Close Encounters of the Third Kind

Contact

Easy Rider

E.T., The Extraterrestrial

Forbidden Planet

Hangar 18

High Strange New Mexico

Independence Day

Invaders From Mars

It Came From Outer Space

It Conquered the World

Men in Black

The Reluctant Astronaut

Roswell

Species

Starman

Stormship Troopers

The Brother From Another Planet

The Day the Earth Stood Still

The Man Who Fell to Earth

The Thing From Another World

The Three Stooges in Orbit

The War of the Worlds

The X-Files

Them!

Waiting for Guffman

index

Abbott, Lee K., 115
Abbott and Costello Go to Mars, 146
Abduction Axioms, 116
abductions, 129
Aboard a Flying Saucer, 79
Above Top Secret (Good), 113
Adamski, George, 105, 116
Adden, Edmond G., 82
Aerial Phenomena Research Organization, 142
Aghasian, Lucille, 65
Air Force Museum, 91; UFO display case at, 92
Albuquerque Journal, description of editorial cartoon from, 70
Albuquerque-Roswell football game, 22
Alfred Hitchcock Presents, 162
Alien, 14, 110, 114, 163; and *Forbidden Planet*, 165
alien abductions, 7, 14, 65–66
Alien Autopsy: Fact or Fiction?, 81, 112–13, 115–16, 117

Alien Chase (5K road race), 68
aliens, 125; accident victim resembles, 93; Air Force denial of storage of, at Wright-Patterson base, 74; and Barnum's mermaid, 109; to be found everywhere, 135; and cover-ups, 124; descriptions of, 109–17; eyes of, 113; gray coloration of, 28, 102, 137; as Japanese, 113; number of digits of, 116; size of, 108. *See also* alien abductions; Generic Alien
Allen, Woody, 5, 25
Amazing Stories, 120, 129
Anderson, Gillian, 109
Anderson, Kurt, 113
Andreasson Affair, The (Fowler), 116
Andrews Air Force Base, 136
android, coining of word, 119
Ankrum, Morris, 148
apparition in tortilla, 60
Area 51 (Nevada), 56, 88, 167
Armstrong, Neil, 85